Uncommon Lives
of
Common Women

the missing half of wisconsin history

by Victoria Brown

in cooperation with
the Commission on the
Status of Women
the Kohler Foundation
the Oscar Mayer Foundation
the Cudahy Foundation

project of the Wisconsin
Feminists Project Fund, Inc.
1975 by Victoria Brown.

Preface

The Wisconsin Feminists Project Fund, Inc. is a non-profit corporation established in 1973 to develop programs benefiting Wisconsin women in their education, employment and social advancement. By January of 1974, the Fund was deeply involved in a statewide training program in women's employment; but this was only the Fund's beginning. The seven members of the Board of WFPF had already begun talking about ways that Wisconsin women could recognize and celebrate the coming Bicentennial *and* International Women's Year. It was their belief that women at all levels should participate in these two events for only through direct participation could women be certain that their stories would be told — and told accurately.

While the Board was discussing ways to tell Wisconsin women's story, I was working on a master's thesis on American women's history at U.W. - Madison. I was a stockholder in the Wisconsin Feminists Project Fund and knew the Board members. When the Board approached me with the idea of a research project on Women in Wisconsin History, I was delighted. I had a job as "project director" — *if* we could raise the money for the project.

Funding is seldom discussed, but it needs to be mentioned here if only to commend those who had the faith (and the courage) to support a fledgling women's history project. I would like to thank the Kohler Foundation and, particularly, Mrs. Linda Karger Kohler for the financial support and personal interest which put this project under way. I would also like to thank the Cudahy Foundation and the Oscar Mayer Foundation for their additional and essential contributions. But above all, I wish to thank the Governor's Commission on the Status of Women for its unending support and its abiding good faith.

It would be impossible for me to thank all the individuals in Wisconsin who helped bring this book into existence. The staff at the Wisconsin State Historical Society in Madison, the staffs of countless local historical societies throughout the state, the many private citizens who took the time and effort to share their stories of Wisconsin women with me, the members of N.O.W. who let me stay in their homes when I traveled around the state — all of these people contributed in very important ways and share my sincere gratitude.

When you are the only person working on a project, the support and interest of those around you is essential. I was fortunate in having a circle of friends and colleagues who took the trouble to understand what I was doing and care about it. Each of them assisted me in ways that were above and beyond the call of duty. For that reason, I give my deepest thanks to Kathryn Clarenbach and Norma Briggs of the Commission on the Status of Women; and to Margo House, Gene Boyer, Judith Kaufman, Ellen Saunders, Carolyn Mueller, Claudia Vlisides, Peter Vlisides, and Susan Mattes of the Wisconsin Feminists Project Fund. Finally, I thank Jim Brown, *not* because he typed the manuscript or did the dishes; but because he gave serious and creative thought to every page in this book.

—Victoria Bissell Brown

Table of Contents

Introduction

This is not a definitive study of women in Wisconsin history. It is an impressionistic collection of short stories — biographies, incidents, quotes, events. Taken together, this wide and varied collection is designed to convey a single message: WOMEN DOING; women being active, being busy, being productive. Whether you read this book from cover-to-cover or randomly, we hope you come away from it with the sense that women in Wisconsin, throughout history and in all walks of life, have been strong, energetic, creative members of their society.

The material included here was selected to give a broad, representative view of Wisconsin women. This is not a history of feminists any more than it is a history of Wisconsin club women or mothers or industrial workers. It is a record of many kinds of common women; women who were fairly typical of their day. Wisconsin's "famous" women are not here. Their stories have been told. It is time to remember that the famous women had a whole population of sisters and that stunning achievement by women has never been confined to a small handful of 'stars'.

Although many of the women included here did do extraordinary things, they were not alone. Even the most extraordinary had counterparts in other communities, other states, other countries. This fact in no way diminishes these women's worth or importance; it simply serves to remind us that what society has insisted upon calling "extraordinary" behavior in a woman has usually been just one of a million possible examples of female strength, courage, and endurance. For even when "woman's place" has been most confined and restricted, woman's energy has still emerged and her strength has endured.

Modern symbols of strength and courage are not usually appropriate for women in the past, of course. Economic independence, educational and professional success, political equality — these were rare for women in Wisconsin history and it would be inaccurate to confine our story to those few women who enjoyed them. To tell women's story accurately, we must broaden our scope; we must look for women's strength and energy within the context of their times. This means taking women where they were at and valuing what they accomplished given the prejudices and requirements of each era.

There are women in this book whose accomplishments could be called "traditionally female". Where this occurs it is simply an honest reflection of the realities of history. In our desire to write a different future for women, it makes no sense to re-write our past. Nor is it necessary. Women have a heritage they can be proud of. It is a heritage of survival, creativity, and growth. This book was written in the belief that to appreciate our survival, we must know what we have endured; to take pride in our creativity, we must know all that we have created; and to understand our growth, we must examine our historic roots.

Because the women in this book are, by definition, "lost women," finding them was the most difficult and challenging part of the research. The search began with a state-wide press release asking Wisconsin citizens to let us know about Wisconsin women. We received well over 100 letters from women and men, telling about their mothers, grandmothers, sisters, aunts, friends, and acquaintances. All of the letters were informative, some were very beautiful. Of the many women we "found" through letters, 20 appear in this book. The other 17 women in the book were found by searching through the Wisconsin history collection at the State Historical Society in Madison, the Manuscript Collection also at the State Historical Society, and various smaller collections at local historical societies and area research centers around the state. Over 250 women were identified in this search as potential candidates for inclusion in the book. That number was narrowed down to 37 on the basis of several considerations; we wanted to be certain that the women selected represented a broad span of Wisconsin's historical eras, geography, ethnic mix, and social and economic life. We also had to be certain that there was enough information available on each woman to write an interesting story.

Women's history is only beginning to be researched and recorded. The most basic footwork is just now being done; as yet there is little data available and few catalogues or guides to material which is available. Wisconsin is fortunate in having a State Historical Society which has collected a large amount of material on women — both local and national. Heightening the value of that collection is the recent publication of a guide to all this material, compiled and written by the Society's Manuscripts Curator, Eleanor McKay.

Still, with all the effort that is now going in to recovering women's past, the task remains a particularly difficult one. Women have been "lost" because male-oriented history never thought it important to study them. Searching for these women now is hampered by the fact that women changed their names with marriage, women often assumed male society's disregard for them and thus failed to record women's history, newspapers did not write many articles — or even obituaries — on women, and local records typically refer to women only in terms of their male relatives. Added to these problems are the problems which all social historians face; the fact that poor people, illiterate people, and ofttimes working people do not have well-documented personal histories. They certainly did not have articles written about them, and if they did write diaries and letters, it is unlikely that they deposited these materials in a historical library. Finally, these groups, like women, have suffered from scholars' disinterest in people's history.

As a result of all the barriers to finding "lost women," this book does not include as many black women, industrial women, and urban working class women as we would have liked. The limits of time, womanpower, and data forced us to take the best of what we could find and hope that this initial effort will inspire others to dig into those areas we overlooked or could not easily penetrate.

The book is organized chronologically, progressing from the 1700's through the 1950's. Interspersed between the 37 biographies are bits and pieces of Wisconsin women's history; a selected sample of events and quotes which are designed to provide historical background and to give a sense of the attitudes and conditions women faced throughout history. We hope these bits and pieces also serve to intensify the feeling that women have been perenially active and involved in their communities.

While this is not a complete collection of Wisconsin women, we hope it reflects certain universal truths about the women of this state and we hope that in some way every daughter's granddaughter can find her mother here.

Part I: Wisconsin's First Women

and the Wisconsin Frontier

In early Indian dialects, the word for wife meant partner, not chattel.[1]

The first Wisconsin women were Native American women — Winnebago in the south and west, Menominee in the north and east, and Chippewa in the far north. We know very little about these tribal women, except that their roles were many and varied, depending on tribal culture and personal circumstances. According to Native American historians Julia Cruikshank and Rosemary Christensen, our society is only now discovering the ways tribal women were misunderstood by the white traders, missionaries, and soldiers who came to Wisconsin in the 18th and 19th centuries.

"When the traders kept accounts of their interactions or observations of Native women, their views reflected the mind-set of the culture from which they came. White women during these trader times were tightly categorized into very definite roles . . . The (white men) did not . . . understand or accept the multi-faceted person that is Indian woman."[2]

Many of the white male settlers married Native women, and while these wives proved to be among the most capable of Wisconsin's early female pioneers, they are not accurate representatives of *tribal* women. In these mixed marriages the Native wife was quickly assimilated into the white society that was developing in Wisconsin territory as early as 1790.

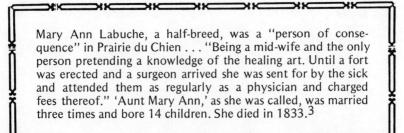

Mary Ann Labuche, a half-breed, was a "person of consequence" in Prairie du Chien . . . "Being a mid-wife and the only person pretending a knowledge of the healing art. Until a fort was erected and a surgeon arrived she was sent for by the sick and attended them as regularly as a physician and charged fees thereof." 'Aunt Mary Ann,' as she was called, was married three times and bore 14 children. She died in 1833.[3]

Electa Quinney

Electa Quinney is generally recognized as Wisconsin's first 'public school' teacher. The school she opened in Kaukana in 1828 was the first in the state where students did not have to pay to be enrolled. Naturally, this meant that many of her pupils were Native Americans and poor whites who had never before been able to afford the luxury of schooling.[4]

Quinney was a Stockbridge-Munsee Indian herself and was particularly interested in teaching the children of the Stockbridge-Munsee settlement around South Kaukana. She had come with her tribe to the Fox River Valley from New York in the massive Indian removal of 1827. The Quinney family was prominent in the Stockbridge-Munsee tribe and must have been fairly prosperous in New York for daughter Electa was educated at primary school in Clinton and at a female seminary in Connecticut — unusual opportunities for an Indian woman at that time.

Before coming to Wisconsin, Quinney put her education to use teaching Indian children in New York. When she arrived in Kaukana she was determined to continue her work by establishing a 'free school' in the nearby Presbyterian mission. Within a few months the school opened its doors. According to one former pupil's recollection, written in 1893, "Miss Quinney was a better teacher than the average teacher today . . . She rarely whipped; opened her school with a prayer. It was modeled after the best public schools of New England at the time."[5]

In a tribute to Quinney in the *Wisconsin Journal of Education* in the 1890's, it was said that "Miss Quinney was highly respected by the whites, and moved in their best society at Fort Howard." It was also said that she refused to marry the sheriff of Brown County because "she was too proud to marry a white man."[6] Instead she married Daniel Adams, a Mohawk, who was a Methodist missionary to the Oneidas. With him she moved to Missouri where he was the pastor for a tribe of Senecas. After his death she married a Cherokee newspaper editor and eventually returned to her farm at Stockbridge, Wisconsin where she died in 1885.

Wisconsin's first white women arrived in the late 18th and early 19th centuries. Usually the relatives of army and government personnel, these first women lived on army forts or government trading posts around Green Bay, Prairie du Chien and Milwaukee. The first civilian pioneer settlement developed in the early 1800's in the southwest lead-mining region around Mineral Point, in Iowa County. By 1836 there were 691 women in Iowa County taking care of 2,317 men and 2,226 children. These settlers were mining land that had previously been mined by Winnebago women.

White settlement was rapid after 1840. Wisconsin's population grew from 31,000 in 1840 to 776,881 in 1860, a jump of 2,400 per cent in 20 years. In contrast to earlier days, the new settlers came as families. They came from New England and the Mid-Atlantic states and, of course, from Germany, Scandanavia, and the British Isles. By 1850, one-third of Wisconsin's people were foreign immigrants.

These settlers came to farm and to work as entrepreneurs, lawyers, editors, preachers, merchants, and politicians. Whatever they came for, their lives were uniformly different. This was especially true for the women for they had many fewer choices about where to go and what to do, fewer contacts with the outside world, greater physical burdens, and often more binding responsibilities. In a recollection of pioneer days in Walworth County, one former settler described the conditions women faced:

"Here there were herds of deer and flocks of wild fowl, the wolf and the sand-hill crane and game, large and small, to give us sport. The lakes and streams abounded in fish and we could take them at our will. There was excitement for us in all this . . . We could roam and fish and hunt as we pleased, amid the freshness and beauties of nature. But how was it for our wives? From all these bright and, to us, fascinating scenes and pastimes, they were excluded. They were shut up with the children in log cabins — when they were fortunate enough to get them — rude huts, often without floors and not infrequently without doors or windows, while the cold, bleak winds of December and March whistled through them. Often they were covered by shakes fastened on with poles . . . Here in one small room filled, perhaps, with smoke; without furniture, except a little of the rudest kind — rough slab stools, an equally rough table and a bedstead, if any, made of poles fastened into the house; without kitchen utensils, save per chance a kettle, a skillet and a frying pan; destitute of crockery and with a little tinware — they were called upon to do, unaided, the duties of a housewife. With these inconveniences and these surroundings they took upon themselves for weeks and months and even years, the burden of their households in a continued struggle with hindrances and perplexities."[7]

Dear Brother and Sister-in-law,   *Summer, 1846*
. . . the vegetables in our garden are growing nicely
. . . They give me great pleasure . . . If I only had a
few good true women friends I would be entirely
satisfied . . .

                     Your faithful sister,
                        Katherine[8]

The Pratt Sisters

Phineas and Betsey Pratt raised six daughters and one son on New York's Lake Ontario coast. In 1838 their eldest daughter, Jane, married Ira Washburn, a steamboat captain. A week later the young couple set off across the lake for the new territory of Wisconsin. Along the way, their steamer hit a storm and they lost most of their belongings. Finally arriving in Wisconsin, the Washburns settled near Beloit and made a home in the wilderness with what little they had left.[9]

Jane's letters home tried to sound cheerful but during those first years she was alone much of the time. Ira was away working on the steamboat to earn a living. As time went on, Jane found the loneliness, the frequent visits from local Indians, the waiting for Ira, and the separation from her sisters hard to endure.

At last in 1844, she persuaded two sisters, Sarah and Susannah, to come for a visit. Sarah was the most educated of the Pratt sisters and perhaps the most introspective. Trained as a schoolteacher, she kept a diary of her long and arduous journey west and of the trials she and her family faced in Wisconsin. According to Sarah's diary, she and Susannah arrived at Jane's home in October of 1844. "I went in without ceremony," wrote Sarah, "and took Jane by surprise. I looked at her but she was so altered I turned my eyes away. I could not bear to see her. She looked so very old. Her eyes were sunk in her head and she had lost so many teeth, it made her face look very different from what she used to be."

In the months and years to come, Sarah recorded the daily tasks and multiple hardships that befell her family. Though plagued by periods of melancholia, Jane continued to perform her duties as a pioneer wife. She was always busy washing, carding and spinning wool, weaving cloth, making soap, picking geese, and baking. During harvest time Jane cooked for fifty men and in all seasons there were travelers stopping at the Washburn cabin for a meal and a night's rest.

Still, Sarah and Susannah knew that Jane was not well and they hesitated to leave her. Both sisters obtained teaching positions in the area and within the year they decided to buy a plot of land and settle near Jane. It was not an easy decision. Sarah had to borrow money to buy the land. Worse, she had to face the fact that she would never be going home.

At about this time, Mr. and Mrs. Pratt decided to move to Wisconsin with their youngest children, Amanda and Collin. Now there were six living in Sarah' s tiny cabin. It was late fall; there was little time to pre- pare the cabin for winter and Mr. Pratt was too old to help with the heavy labor. Mrs. Pratt and sister Amanda were ill upon arrival. Within weeks, Jane Pratt Washburn gave birth to her fourth baby, Mrs. Pratt and Amanda worsened, and Sarah and Susannah found themselves traveling many miles between cabins to nurse their relatives. Sarah had to give up her teaching and take in sewing to earn a little money.

Sarah wrote in November, 1845, "I can truly say it has been a time of more anxiety than I ever realized . . . I feel at times quite lonely and feel the need of counsel, and we have no opportunity to attend church and have had none since our people got here."

The winter closed in. "It is a very solemn time to think of the sick- ness around Wisconsin," wrote Sarah during the fever of 1846. Ira Washburn took sick, along with two of the Washburn sons and Collin Pratt. Sarah, too, was struck. "My cough seems to increase. We were all quite sick and sister Susannah had plenty to do. She was broke of rest very much in waiting on the sick and it was a wonderment to me that she kept round as she did." By fall, Susannah was in a sick bed and "though far from being well," old Mrs. Pratt was nursing her children.

A fifth sister, Semanthe, arrived to help with the nursing and life went on as best it could. Amanda married in the spring of 1847. "She left the house with tears," wrote Sarah, "but what was the cause, I did not inquire. I felt within my heart that if I were in her place, about to leave a parental home to cast my lot with one that might prove unkind, I too should feel some degree of tender feelings. I wish them success and happiness. But I am too tired to write today."

Sarah never recovered from her illness. She died in September of 1847, at the age of 28. A week before her death, her father died of the same fever. Mrs. Pratt lived out her life in Sarah's cabin. The younger sisters married and moved away. Jane's sanity was permanently marred by the disease and death of the winter of 1846. Susannah wrote later, "Jane's sickness was hard for me to overcome . . . I often felt there was nothing sure but death and it is much easier to see one dead than insane."

ᘛᘔᘛᘔᘛᘔᘛᘔᘛᘔᘛᘔᘛᘔᘛᘔᘛᘔᘛᘔᘛᘔ

Dear Family,   *March 23, 1842*
Last night Mrs. Wheeler gave birth to a dead child. She had been confined to her bed for two months previously, on account of convulsions and other dif- ficulties. Again I must speak of the great necessity for women missionaries to this country to be of good and firm health. None should come but of strong and rugged constitution if they wish to be of use.
Florantha Sproat,
LaPointe, Wisconsin[10]

Susan and Henry Gratiot were living the refined life of St. Louis 'aristocrats' when Henry was appointed government agent to the Winnebago Indians . . . right at the start of the Black Hawk War. In 1827, the Gratiots moved their five children to the Wisconsin frontier, settling at Gratiots Grove, two miles from Shullsburg and 20 miles from Galena.[11]

Already the war had sent one Shullsburg teacher fleeing with her students to safety, and subsequent attempts to keep school open during the war failed.[12] But a cultured woman like Susan Gratiot was not about to watch her children grow up uneducated in the wilds of Wisconsin. So determined was she to hold school, that in 1834 she rented her own cabin to two teachers from Galena so they could run a boarding school at Gratiots Grove. Mr. and Mrs. Gratiot moved in to a one-room apartment in Galena, leaving their daughters at the boarding school. Mrs. Gratiot wrote to her brother of the move:

"None but a parent . . . can enter into our feeling. We had no school since May. Susan and Mary had taken hold with a determination to learn. I could not think of sending them to Galena . . . and by giving up our place we send all to school . . . it is a great relief to me to know that they are at a place where they can learn . . . I have not had time to write . . . This move has been equal to an Indian War."[13]

Marion Johnson Cooper

When Marion Johnson Cooper moved to Wisconsin with her brothers in 1842, she brought with her a wealth of skills that would prove invaluable on the frontier. The seventh child in a family of 10, Marion Johnson grew up in the rolling hill country of central Massachusetts. For a woman, she was extraordinarily fortunate in receiving both an education in the homemaking skills such as weaving, cooking, and sewing, as well as a formal education in reading, writing, arithmetic, literature and music. She attended "select school" (high school) and taught for a while before setting off with her brothers on a schooner bound for Milwaukee.[14]

It did not take Marion Johnson long to find a teaching position in the town of Greenfield (now West Allis) and she taught for almost two years, until she met and married John Cooper, the postmaster at Greenfield. Marion Cooper did not continue teaching after marriage, but she had plenty to do. From the day she married until the day she died, Cooper's house was full of people. John's parents lived in the Cooper home until their deaths and Marion Cooper bore seven children in her first 13 years of marriage. Two of the children died in infancy, two were but 18 months apart.

In between caring for her home, her in-laws, her children and the hired help, Marion Cooper ran the post office while her postmaster husband ran the farm. Having the post office meant that the Cooper home was the center of activity in western Milwaukee County. The stage came through every day carrying mail that had to be distributed and passengers that had to be refreshed with a cold drink and a comfortable chair. Then, too, came all the local residents to claim their mail, read the magazines and newspapers that had not yet been claimed by others, and to talk with Marion Cooper.

Since the Cooper home was near the school, the teacher boarded with them much of the time. And since John Cooper was the Territorial Justice, their parlor was the scene of countless weddings, will-readings and minor squabbles. All these activities were, of course, in addition to the Coopers' basic responsibilities for running the farm and providing food and clothing for themselves and their children.

None of these duties ever seemed to bother Marion Cooper — except once, in her second year of marriage, when John Cooper was appointed as a delegate to the Legislative Committee of the Constitutional Convention of 1846. It was a great honor to be part of the formation of the new state of Wisconsin, but all of the time John spent on public affairs added to Marion's load on the farm and at the post office. The convention began in October, during fall harvest, and lasted until spring. Marion's letters during this period plead for John's return. These letters portray a couple who shared their work and their worries. They tell us that in John's absence, Marion had to manage the harvesting of the potato crop and 400 apple trees, not to mention tending the cabbages, beets, squash, and pumpkins, the turkeys, hens, geese, and chickens, the sheep and pigs, the Coopers' two young sons, and the five hired loggers who cut timber all day and required great quantities of food, a place to sleep, and clean clothes.

Marion Cooper maintained herself and her home at this pace for 25 years. The Coopers managed the post office until 1869 when Marion Cooper died, at the age of 53. After her death, John Cooper gave up his job as postmaster; he could not handle the work alone.

The state Constitutional Convention of 1846 considered two radical proposals for women's rights: first, that married women should have independent property rights; second, that all women should have the vote.

The proposal for woman suffrage was, it turned out, a joke made in response to those who wanted to grant Negroes and Indians the franchise. In an apparent attempt at sarcasm, certain delegates sought to deny non-white males their suffrage by tying it to the ridiculous idea of woman suffrage. After much heated debate, the whole proposal was discarded and only white males were granted the vote.[15]

By contrast, the provision for married women's property rights was considered quite seriously at the convention. An article finally incorporated into the 1846 constitution read, in part, "All property real and personal, of the wife, owned by her at the time of her marriage, and also that acquired by her afterword . . . otherwise than from her husband shall be her separate property."

According to most observers, it was this provision for married women's property rights, along with a controversial banking law, that caused Wisconsin voters to reject the constitution of 1846. When the constitution of 1848 was presented to the electorate, it contained no mention of married women's property rights . . . and it was adopted. But in 1850, less than two years later, a law was passed which gave married women the right to own and control their own property.[16]

Mariette Huntly Snell

Mariette Huntly Snell was one of the first married women in Wisconsin to own property in her own name.[17] A native of Lyme, Connecticut, Snell had come to Wisconsin in 1838 with her husband, Erastus. They came by boat from New York, landing at Milwaukee, and according to local history Mariette Snell was the only woman in the group to walk the entire distance from Milwaukee to their new home at Ft. Atkinson.[18]

Actually, the Snells blazed a trail seven miles farther west of Ft. Atkinson to Red Cedar Lake where they staked a claim on the lake shore and built a crude shelter with no windows and a blanket for a door. Later, they bought 100 acres on that site from the government and built a large, sturdy home. Erastus Snell was a day laborer in Ft. Atkinson, walking into town on Monday morning and returning home on Saturday night. Left alone during the week, Mariette Snell took care of the property and livestock and the six children she bore between 1840 and 1854. By 1840, Mrs. Snell was also running an inn in her home. She called the inn the Red Cedar Lake House and as it was a regular stopping place for the stage coach en route from Milwaukee to Madison, Mariette Snell did a brisk business.[19]

As time passed, both Erastus and Mariette Snell prospered. With his savings, Erastus Snell purchased an additional 160 acres and was able to stop working in town and devote himself to farming. Mariette Snell also decided to purchase 160 acres with her savings. It was upon purchase of this land in 1855 that Mariette Snell petitioned the legislature to have the title put in her name. As she explained in her petition, she had earned the money herself and she wanted to own the land herself. Mariette Snell continued to prosper as an inn-keeper until her death in 1877.

Mrs. Ocshner Manz came to Buffalo County from Nanikon, Switzerland with 18 others in May, 1851. She was so effective at curing sick people that when a doctor tried to sue her for practicing without a license, he was run out of town.[20]

The temperance movement in Wisconsin was conducted by three main groups: the Anti-Saloon League, the most fanatical wing of the movement; the Women's Christian Temperance Union, the most famous and most broadly reform-minded wing; and the Good Templars, the oldest and most conservative wing. Women are usually associated with the W.C.T.U. which, at its height, was led by a Wisconsin woman, Frances Willard. But women were also active in the ax-waving Anti-Saloon League (Carrie Nation was a Fond du Lac member), and the staid Good Templars.[21]

Emma Brown

"From our brother's grave we come back to take up our burdens alone — to work in the cause to which we have both given the best years of our lives. And while we cannot make the *Chief* what it has been with his ready pen, yet we trust it will still do good service." Thus wrote Emma Brown on May 15, 1865 upon the death of her brother, Thurlow. Emma and Thurlow Brown had been putting out a temperance newspaper together since 1846. Emma had gone to work for Thurlow at the age of 19, "to save him the cost of an extra hand." Now, twenty years later, she found herself the sole proprietor, editor and publisher of *The Wisconsin Chief*, the unofficial organ of the Wisconsin Good Templars.[22]

The *Chief* was a sometimes-weekly, sometimes-monthly four-page sheet whose motto was "Right On!" It was devoted to upholding the ideal of temperance and exposing the evils of drink. The paper actually began as the *Cayuga Chief* in the Browns' native New York, but they moved to Ft. Atkinson, Wisconsin in 1856 and established the *Chief* as Ft. Atkinson's first newspaper. According to Emma Brown's recounting, "No paper ever met with fiercer opposition than the *Chief* in the first two decades. Faction after faction tried the crushing out process. Many a time it has seemed almost an impossibility to get out another number." Still, perhaps miraculously, the paper kept appearing — for the first nine years with Thurlow as publisher and Emma as editor; for the next 24 years with Emma Brown working alone as publisher and editor. During her last ten years alone, Brown not only wrote, edited and distributed the *Chief*, but set the type as well.[23]

The *Chief* did change under Emma Brown's hand. She was not given to the lengthy editorial tirades against 'rum dealers' and 'liquor lobbyists' that were Thurlow's specialty. Emma Brown's *Chief* carried more reform pieces; syndicated articles on prison conditions and factory conditions, and many more articles on women's rights. Brown believed, as did most women in the temperance movement, that women were the ultimate victims of intemperance because they were legally powerless against drunken husbands and fathers. Most states at this time gave men total control of women's property, wages and children. Brown's desire that women be allowed to escape such dependency is reflected in news articles and editorials, such as the one dated June 19, 1869:

"We were gratified a few days since to learn that Miss Mary Car-michael, a lady qualified in every respect for the position, had been appointed and sworn in as Deputy Registrar of Deeds for Monroe County. Miss Carmichael is just as well qualified for such a position as any man, and if there is any impropriety in her having the office, we fail to detect it."

In addition to her work on the *Chief*, Brown was a "faithful servant" for the Wisconsin Good Templars, serving as "Grand Vice Templar" and representative to the state's "Grand Lodge" from Ft. Atkinson. When she learned that she had cancer in February, 1889, Brown dissolved the *Wisconsin Chief* — which was, by then, the oldest temperance news-paper in the country — and shifted her subscription lists to another temperance paper in Wisconsin. But she kept working for the Lodge. In a letter she admitted, "I ought to have stopped sooner, but I could do the work so much easier than one not used to it."

Emma Brown died in June of 1889 in Madison. At the time, a Good Templar convention was being held in Chicago and upon word of her death Wisconsin's Grand Chief Templar ordered that every lodge in the state be draped in mourning for three months.

Christina Wallberg Kumlien

Thure Kumlien is widely known as one of the finest pioneer natura-lists of the 19th century. What is less widely known is that Kumlien came to this country from a wealthy Swedish background, bringing no skills for survival in the wilderness and little interest in farming the forty acres he bought on the shores of Lake Koshkonong. Standing between Kumlien and starvation on the Wisconsin frontier were his wife, Christina, and his sister-in-law, Sophia Wallberg.[24]

This is not to say that Thure Kumlien did not try to succeed as a Jefferson County farmer. But he himself admitted that neither his sheltered life as a Swedish aristocrat nor his education at Upsala Uni-versity had prepared him for the heavy labor that was required to survive in Wisconsin. By contrast, Christina and Sophia, two of the eleven children of a low-ranking Swedish cavalry officer, were raised to work hard. Their only education was in domestic science and before coming to America they worked as maids for wealthy Swedish families.

Thure met and fell in love with Christina when he was visiting friends at the country estate where she was a maid. Knowing that an aristocrat and a serving girl would never be allowed to marry in Sweden, they 'escaped' to America with Christina's sister, Sophia, as chaperone.

Arriving in Wisconsin in 1843, the newly-wed Kumliens staked out a claim on Lake Koshkonong. Their site was near other Swedish set-tlers, but was also in the path of one of North America's principle bird migration routes for Thure had decided to use his love of orni-thology to study the as-yet-unrecorded activities of southern Wisconsin birds.

Sophia Wallberg always called the Kumlien farm 'home,' but she worked out for periods of time at other homes in the area that needed a midwife, nurse, or housekeeper. Her earnings from this work were often contributed to the Kumlien household.

Christina Kumlien ran that household — as well as working by Thure's side on the farm. A journal kept by Thure between 1843 and 1853 records that, "Christina helped me saw pieces for windows and doors upstairs," "Christina and I put up twelve cocks of hay," "Christina and I cut nine bushels of wheat," "Christina and I butcher two pigs," "Christina and I made a log barrel of good dimensions," "Christina moulded candles," etc.[25]

The journal shows that while Thure was working hard on the farm, he was also devoting much of his energy and interest to nature study. When others might be out cutting hay, Thure was off searching for specimens in the fields, the marshes and the tops of trees. And the more time Thure spent on his birds, the more time Christina had to spend maintaining the farm and the household. Between 1853 and 1859, Christina bore four children — three boys and a girl — which only added to her responsibilities.[26]

Thure did not earn a salary as a naturalist until 1867 when he began teaching at Albion Academy a few miles from the farm. Meanwhile, his reputation was growing; students and ornithologists from all over the world came to visit at the Kumlien farm. Christina fed them all, housed the few she could fit in their small log cabin and, of course, managed the farm so Thure would be free to do his work.

It would be a mistake to read resentment or denial into this story. Christina Wallberg Kumlien was a woman of her time. The work she did was fulfilling because it was essential and was done in a partnership. Indeed, Christina considered herself quite fortunate to be married to a man she loved and who loved her. The life she led was the only life she knew and there is no evidence that she ever dreamt of anything different. The one thing she did dream of was a frame house. And in the summer of 1874, when Thure was earning decent money as a naturalist, the Kumliens were able to start building Christina's house. When the house was well under way, Christina became very ill. She was confined to her bed for several weeks and nursed by Sophia, but it was no use. She died of stomach cancer in September, 1874 shortly before her house was completed. After her death, Thure wrote to a friend, "I am but a shadow of what I have been — take interest in nothing and do my work in a kind of machine-like way . . . The attachment that bound my wife to me . . . seems somehow to have grown stronger with age."

"In the early days of the Oschwald Community, every ablebodied woman had a job to do, either working in the fields or at a trade . . . During the winter, husbands often worked in logging camps in Northern Wisconsin leaving their wives and children to fend for themselves. Women learned to hitch up a team of horses or oxen, to milk a cow, mend fences, shoot a gun, butcher a rabbit or a wild bird. If they were widowed or abandoned they plowed a field or operated a store to support themselves and their children. Determination made almost anything possible."[27]

*IN RECOGNITION OF WOMANHOOD: Their
Role in Manitowoc County History*

Part II: The Civil War

and Wisconsin Women

Wisconsin participated enthusiastically in the American Civil War of 1861-1865. The state's immigrant population felt great sympathy for the Southern slaves and the Yankee population was politically committed to the burgeoning Republican Party. For several years before the war, Wisconsin had been known as a safe refuge for runaway slaves on their way to Canada. The Wisconsin Supreme Court even defied federal law by declaring the Fugitive Slave Law null and void within the state boundaries.

On the eve of war in 1861, Wisconsin had 1,992 volunteers in the state militia. By the end of the war in 1865, 82,000 Wisconsin men had been in service — roughly one out of every nine Wisconsin citizens. Over 12,000 of these men died; nearly one in seven of those involved.[28]

The Civil War affected American women — and Wisconsin women — in several ways. The war years found many women working alone on farms, in factories, and in stores to put food on the table and clothes on their children's backs. It was up to these women to keep the family farm or business going until their husbands, fathers, sons or brothers returned. And many did not return. Thousands of women were made permanently independent by the war; the sole breadwinners for their families.

This dramatic and widespread shift in women's economic responsibilities coincided with the growing political importance of the Women's Rights Movement. The movement had begun in the 1850's but gained great momentum during the Civil War when patriotic women learned abruptly that the country's men did not want women to serve, to advise, or to vote. Women everywhere were radicalized by the war experience. It taught them that they *could* stand on their own, but that laws and customs prevented them.

Many of the most famous leaders in the Women's Rights Movement visited Wisconsin in the 1860's and 70's, leaders like Elizabeth Cady Stanton, Susan B. Anthony, Lucy Stone, and Antoinette Blackwell Brown. They encouraged Wisconsin women to fight for their rights to an education, employment and a political voice. Progress was made in those early years. Women began attending Wisconsin colleges and universities — though these once-male bastions were openly reluctant. Economic necessity, supported by political conviction, kept many Wisconsin women at work in previously "male" occupations after the war — though many were fired as soon as the men came home. And the battle for a political voice — the Wisconsin woman suffrage movement — grew slowly but steadily, until it could no longer be ignored.

Ella Hobart was a temperance lecturer during the Civil War, raising money for the Wisconsin Soldier's Aid Society. In 1864, she learned that her estranged husband, Reverend John Hobart, had been dismissed from service for being absent without leave. Ella Hobart immediately applied for his position as chaplain of the First Wisconsin Heavy Artillery. She accompanied the First to Camp Alexandria where she functioned as a regular Army chaplain, with one exception: she received no pay. Secretary of War Stanton refused to recognize her appointment as chaplain and Governor Fairchild declined to press her case. After the war, Ella Hobart fought for compensation and for disability pay for the malaria she contracted while in service. But she went to her death never recognized or recompensed for her service as a Civil War chaplain.[29]

Eliza T. Wilson was the first woman in western Wisconsin to volunteer as a Civil War nurse. Upon her return from service with the Fifth Wisconsin Infantry, Wilson bought land outside of Eau Claire where she ran a successful farm and milling operation. Being "independent in thought and action, she conducted her business affairs with ability and good judgement."[30] Known as a supporter of women's rights, Wilson hosted Elizabeth Cady Stanton and Susan B. Anthony when they visited Eau Claire during their first trip to Wisconsin in 1869.[31]

"Many a man was in the field cradling down his grain when he had to drop his scythe and go to war. If he had a family, they carried on from where he left off, because they had to eat . . . Need is a hard taskmaster, but the women met and beat it . . . they carried on and got their small fields plowed and sowed the following spring."[32]

AN IMMIGRANT'S MEMORIES

In December of 1861, the Board of Richland County levied a tax of $2,500 to be used for families of volunteers . . . But before a woman could get a share of the money, she had to swear she was a pauper.[33]

Mary Schaal Johns

"I was married when I was 17 just to get a home. My husband was 26 and just a year over from Germany. He was a cooper by trade and opened a shop in Iron Mountain. Three children were born to us and we moved to Oakfield. Then the American Civil War broke out.

"Everything was excitement . . .my husband felt he must go and help free the slaves in the South . . .I felt very bad, but I was willing that my husband should go, because I thought the slaves should be free. We had just built us a five-room cottage but the upstairs was still unplastered. My husband left me with this cottage, a cow, a few chickens, and three children, the eldest a little over four years old.

"The next three years were hard for us. Six months after my husband left, a fourth baby was born to me. . . I had to saw and split my own wood. On rainy days, I brought the sticks in the kitchen, and laid them, one at a time, with the ends resting on two chairs, while I sawed them in two. I would set a child on each end of the stick to hold it steady . . . There were very few men left in the country, except old men and cripples. All the able-bodied men had gone to war. The old men and women ran the farms.

"Once a month I had to go seven miles for the $5.00 the county gave me for support as a soldier's wife . . .Often I did not get back until long after dark. My eldest child was as yet only six, and was sickly. I had to leave her all day with the other three. She used to put a candle in the window so I could see it on my return.

"My sister had a store in Mayville and once a week she drove over with denim cloth to make overalls. I had no sewing machine, but I was able to make one pair a day by doing my housework after dark, by candle light. I got 50¢ a pair for the overalls.

"News of big battles came. My husband was in Murphysboro, Chattanooga, Atlanta, and marched with Sherman to the sea. We had always written each other once a week, but now all news of Sherman's army ceased and I heard nothing for weeks. When a letter came from my husband, I used to put it under my pillow and pray to Father to not let my babes become orphans as I had been. When I nursed my baby, the hot tears rolled down my cheeks.

"Still with Sherman, my husband marched to Washington, and was mustered out. He came home by way of Milwaukee . . .When he got to the station, he started right out for our cottage . . . I had just lain down when the train pulled in, and the children ran in to say, "There is a soldier coming." A moment after that, my husband came in with the children clinging to him. . . Then for one time in my life, I fainted."[34]

—By Mary Schaal Johns, as told to the Reverend Gilbert Wilson in 1915. Johns immigrated from Germany with her family at age 10. Orphaned at age 12, she worked for families in the Mayville area to earn her room and board.

During the Civil War, Wisconsin women filled many jobs left vacant by soldiers, particularly in shops and factories. Before the war there were only 773 women in the state employed as shopkeepers or factory workers. By 1870 that figure had risen five times, to 3,967.[35]

The printing trade felt the scarcity of labor early in the Civil War for printers enlisted at a rate disproportionate to their numbers. Women were hired to fill their posts — at *half* the male printers' pay — and the women quickly became as skillful as their predecessors. In 1863, Milwaukee Typographical Union No. 23 protested the hiring of female typesetters at the *Milwaukee Sentinel* and when management refused to respond, the male printers went out on strike. There was strong sympathy for the *Sentinel* management who argued that they were only doing their patriotic duty by giving employment to women left dependent by the war. The strike was settled but women were phased out of the printing offices as soon as the war ended.[36]

Letitia Abbott Wall

Letitia Abbott Wall was a Southern belle. Born in 1829 and raised on a North Carolina plantation, she spent her girlhood surrounded by indulgent parents, negro servants, fancy clothes, gay parties, and ardent suitors. She could have had her pick of men from the local gentry, but instead she chose the "tall and fine-looking" Alpheus Wall, a pioneer farmer from Missouri. She went off with Alpheus to the Wisconsin frontier in 1853. In doing so she cut herself off from her family and her home forever.[37]

Alpheus Wall was, by his own admission, "somehow or other, no 'count." Letitia Wall soon recognized that any income they required for survival would have to be earned by her hand. Joseph Schafer, a Wisconsin historian who grew up near 'Aunt 'Titia' in the valleys of the Blue River and Fennimore Creek, recalled the dignity with which she conducted her life:

"With her the hope of prosperity, if it had been experienced at all, faded early. She knew perfectly well that her slender living must come out of her earnings . . .Out of them, too, must come the weekly allowance of whisky and tobacco for Alpheus . . .But no one would think of commiserating with Aunt 'Titia . . .It wouldn't do to insinuate to 'Titia

that her husband was shiftless, as they would have done with others, for 'Titia was different. And being different, being what she was — a strong, self-respecting and proud woman — she made the entire neighborhood aware that such virtues not only existed but were worthy of high respect."

Although she was not trained in many fields, Wall was very skilled in the arts of spinning, weaving, quilting and needlework. The neighboring farms had sheep for wool and Wall soon convinced a group of women to buy a large spinning wheel which she taught them to use. At the same time, she procured a loom for herself and went into business weaving cloth out of the wool spun and dyed by her neighbors.

During the Civil War, when cloth was in terribly short supply, Wall did a decent local business. With the war over, the demand for cloth-weaving declined. Wall turned to carpet-weaving. Many farmers were moving out of their original log cabins and into frame houses; Wall supplied these new homes with the rag carpets then in demand. This occupation allowed Wall to support herself and her husband. But it was not a large or steady income, reports Schafer:

Wisconsin State Historical Society

"She knew that if the farmers' crops failed they could get along without her kind of carpets. On the other hand, with a little more prosperity, ingrain carpets would come in and her occupation as a weaver of rag carpets would be gone. Want was never more than a few weeks behind her . . .(still) she had the true spirit of craftsmanship, taking satisfaction in doing her work well."

Wall seldom left her own cottage but she was a central source of information for the community. Well-read and up-to-date, it was said that she could out-talk and out-argue any man in the area on political questions. At the same time, she knew the birthdays, wedding days, courtships and break-ups of everyone in the valley and could discern the most subtle nuances of people's lives from aimless talk.

Alpheus Wall lived to a fairly ripe old age, but after he died — leaving Letitia Wall free from the burden of supporting him — she seemed to give up. She entered a home for aged women run by the Order of the Eastern Star in 1901 and died there at the age of 83.

Ann Bicknell Ellis

There were only a handful of blacks residing in Wisconsin before the Civil War and these few were concentrated in Milwaukee. After the war, many freed slaves came north to Wisconsin where they knew there had been an outspoken Abolition movement and an active underground railway. One of the ways blacks came north was as an employee of a white Northerner. Such was the case with Ann Bicknell Ellis. Born into slavery in the 1850's, she escaped with her mother and brother to Cairo, Illinois during the war. There she was 'found' by Dr. Simon Bicknell, an Army surgeon, and sent north to his home in Ft. Atkinson. (Ann's mother was given a job at the hospital in Cairo.)[39]

We know very little about Ann Ellis' life in Ft. Atkinson except that she earned her living as a candy-maker and married a black man named Jim Ellis in 1875. Jim Ellis had also been brought to Ft. Atkinson by Dr. Bicknell and he and Ann were the only two black people in the town. The few newspaper clippings that exist on them express great pride in the fact that the Ellis' lived pleasant, undisturbed lives in Ft. Atkinson. According to these clips, they were fully integrated into the community. One oft-repeated story told of a southern couple visiting in Ft. Atkinson who refused to sit in church because the Ellis' were seated in a front pew. According to the story, the visitors were sharply rebuked by their hosts and the congregation.

The Ellis' apparently prospered in Ft. Atkinson. For her part, Ann Ellis supplied the

town with its candy. Jim, meanwhile, worked as a postman and carpenter. The house that Jim Ellis built for his family was right across the road from the high school — an ideal location for a candy-maker. Ann was able to make candy in the morning and sell it right out of her kitchen after school.

Working at home also allowed Ann to tend to her two sons. Though one of the sons died at age two, the other son, Clark, grew to manhood and tried to live in Ft. Atkinson after he married a black woman from the South. But his young wife felt isolated in all-white Ft. Atkinson and the couple soon moved away. We have no way of knowing the extent of Ann Ellis' own isolation as the only black woman in a northern rural community. All that remains of her personal effects is an unmailed postcard dated 1913, two years after Jim's death and one year before her own. The card is from Ann Ellis to Miss Mabel Dinning in Madison and says simply, "It's so lonely here."

Coeducation at UW

When the University of Wisconsin - Madison opened its doors in 1850, the Regents announced a plan to admit women to its Normal Department (teacher-training course). But little was done about the plan until 1857 when the Regents, encouraged by the success of coeducational experiments at other eastern and midwestern schools, pledged that U.W. would meet the needs of those who wished to send their daughters there. By 1860, thirty of the 50 graduates from the Normal Department were women.[40]

The Civil War so depleted the male student body at Madison that 15 women in the Normal Department were allowed to take 'regular' courses — just to keep up enrollment. By 1865, 18 women were enrolled in a "select course" which meant simply that, as students, they were taking a regular curriculum; but, as women, they were listed in the Normal Department. The University's reorganization of 1866 looked like the final victory for coeducation; under it "The University and all its departments and colleges shall be open alike to male and female students." But when the presidency of the University was offered to Paul Chadbourne in 1867 he demanded that coeducation be modified as a condition of his accepting the job. Chadbourne claimed that a coeducational institution would not receive the status, public confidence, or financial support required to succeed.

Under Chadbourne's three-year administration, the Normal Department was replaced by a 'Female College.' This separate college had no separate curriculum or requirements; it simply had separate recitations. Thus, during Chadbourne's three years at U.W., professors were required to give two separate lectures; one to the men and one to the women. This obviously inefficient and expensive system of segregation was abolished by Chadbourne's successors, John Twombly and John Bascom, both advocates of complete coeducation at U.W.

"When Paul Ansel Chadbourne was President of the University of Wisconsin, I was living at South Hall. My rooms were on the second floor, and consisted of a sitting room and two bedrooms, accommodating four students. Our windows looked toward North Hall and east toward the City of Madison. Our simple furniture was mostly brought from our homes.

"Our college was called 'Female College.' We soon understood that our President was not in favor of coeducation. Our recitations were entirely separate from the gentlemen, and when Commencement Day arrived, the ladies received their diplomas on the Tuesday before the Gentlemen received theirs. The "Gentlemen's Commencement" was held in the State Capitol, the "Ladies'" in the Old Congregational Church."[41]

by Edna Phillips Chynoweth, a founding member of the Women's International League for Peace and Freedom in Madison in the 1920's.

In 1901, Ladies' Hall was renamed Chadbourne Hall in honor of the man who had been instrumental in its construction but would have had little sympathy with its ultimate use.

"The women lacked gymnasium drill or any form of organized athletics, except that sometime in 1878 or 1879 . . .the inadequate University gymnasium (by custom ceded to the men exclusively) was opened to the women a few hours every week. This was far from sufficient exercise, and the women suffered from lack of regular exercise unless they indulged individually in swimming, boating, or riding. There was little enough of this, but the feat of swimming from Picnic Point to our boathouse was accomplished by a woman in my class. It is an interesting manifestation of the attitude of certain public critics toward change, that when the collegiate training of women was first on trial there were clamorous complaints that the health of young women was being wrecked; now the same class of public critics are loudly complaining that college women are 'Amazons'."42

"The University in 1874-1887,"
by Florence Bascom, daughter
of U.W. President John Bascom.

Wisconsin State Historical Society
Students at the University of Wisconsin — Madison, 1895-96

Clarissa Tucker Tracy

Clarissa Tucker Tracy joined the faculty at Ripon College in 1859 when the school was little more than a charter and a name. She remained on the staff for 46 years serving as teacher, administrator and campus "housemother."[43]

Tracy was not originally employed at Ripon as a teacher but, rather, as "matron of the boarding department." Despite her 20 years of teaching experience and her expertise in botany, Tracy was hired to be the school's housekeeper. There is no record to tell how she altered this arrangement, but by 1871 Tracy was teaching a full load of classes in Algebra, Arithmetic, English Literature, Composition, Latin and Botany, in addition to performing her duties as college "matron."

As matron, Tracy was in charge of meals and rooms for over 100 people. There was little money so there was little equipment and no hired staff. Tracy's own salary in those early years was dependent upon her ability to economize in the domestic department. In order to have any staff, she had to train and supervise student helpers both in the kitchen and in the boarding house.

From the descriptions of her written by former students and colleagues, it would appear that Tracy was a cool and meticulously organized administrator in the kitchen and an inspiring but rigorous taskmaster in the classroom. She was most intense in her work as a botanist. In 1889 she published a thorough catalogue of "Plants Growing Without Cultivation in Ripon and the Near Vicinity," and was often heard to say that she could not understand how anyone could analyze a flower and ever forget the analysis. So great was her own passion for flowers that she once confessed to analyzing the flowers on the ladies' bonnets in church, "and was only recalled to the absurdity of what I was doing by finding so many essential parts missing."

Obviously, cool administration and skilled teaching did not, alone, earn for Tracy the personal accolades that came to her both before and after her death. Tracy's strength and efficiency were accompanied by a warmth and sensitivity that always made her approachable. One student recalled that, "though the duties were many and arduous, she seemed always to have time for helping students with their lessons or with soul problems . . . She was always at her post . . . I never knew her to have even a headache or indisposition of any kind . . . though she frequently rose at four o'clock in the morning to get her bakings done."

Tracy had always wanted to teach in a 'frontier setting' like Ripon. Born and raised in Pennsylvania, she taught school from the age of 14 in order to earn money for her own education. She was a student at Troy Seminary in 1844 when she fell in love with Horace Tracy and married him, despite his delicate health. The Tracy's were married for four years and had two children before Horace Tracy died. Three years later their daughter died and Clarissa Tracy was left to raise her young son alone. After several years of teaching in Pennsylvania, Tracy decided to fulfill her dream of teaching in "less favored places," and set off with 10-year-old Horace Jr. to work in Wisconsin. Soon after, she joined the staff at Ripon. During her 46 years there, she was an active member of the Congregational Church and the W.C.T.U., and served as the sponsor of Dawes Cottage, a female students' off-campus living co-op which was as successful as it was revolutionary.

Tracy moved off-campus herself in 1893 but continued to tutor students and attend faculty meetings as Professor Emeritus until a few weeks before her death in 1905. Of her many eulogies, perhaps the best recalled Tracy as "a center of moral and intellectual unity through the years . . . a cable of steel in a difficult pass."

On October 8, 1871 the Great Peshtigo Fire broke out in Marinette County burning over a half dozen counties in north-eastern Wisconsin, killing hundreds of people and destroying valuable timber and farmland. News of the fire did not reach Madison until October 10 when Governor Lucius Fairchild and all the state's officials were in Chicago aiding victims of that city's great fire.

A capitol clerk took the telegram from Peshtigo to the Governor's wife, Frances Bull Fairchild, who immediately swung into action. For two days, 24-year-old Frances Fairchild acted as governor of the state.

She commandeered a boxcar loaded with supplies bound for Chicago, ordered railroad officials to give it priority over all other traffic, and upon discovering that the car contained food and clothing but no defenses against the October cold, she rallied Madison women to stuff blankets into the already loaded car. After the car was dispatched, Fairchild issued a public appeal for money, clothing, bedding and supplies, with the result that a second boxcar left Madison that night.[44]

Elizabeth Stone

"She always carried to the sickbed a round, yellow tin box. In it she kept moldy bread, each scrap of bread being added when it was no longer usable for table. The dust from opening the box was a cloud of green. When she dressed a wound she made poultices from this bread and warm milk or water . . . This she applied directly to the wound and the healing was rapid and clean. Whether she went by carriage, sled, horseback or by walking, she carried this tin with her. In all the years of her service, she never lost a timber-related patient."[45]

Elizabeth Robinson Stone was using penicillin to treat victims of timber accidents in Peshtigo, Wisconsin 70 years before Dr. Alexander Fleming "discovered" it. Stone was a farm wife but she had begun practical nursing during the Civil War and continued to assist the

sick and injured wherever and whenever she was called. Though she had no formal training in medicine, Stone took up nursing because "she had a gentle touch and found that it was needed." The War found Stone living in Chilton, Wisconsin. The Army had called up all the community's doctors and in their absence Stone nursed many of her neighbors.

After the War, the Stones farmed in Chilton and then Peshtigo, settling finally in Pardeeville in 1877. Wherever they farmed, Mrs. Stone was able to supplement the family's income with her work as a practical nurse. Though she did not charge a fee for her services, patients often repaid her with goods and produce.

Elizabeth Stone cared for the sick as long as she lived. Dr. Chandler of Pardeeville used to say that she had delivered as many babies as he. Unfortunately, she was less successful with her own health than she was with others'. Four of her eight children died at birth and she herself died of shingles, "a malady for which her precious moldy bread would have no effect." She never knew that her mold discovery would one day be a manufactured medicine. All she knew was that it worked. The mold, combined with her special touch made Elizabeth Stone a successful practitioner in a primitive period of medical history.

Dr. Laura Ross of Milwaukee was one of the West's first women doctors. Dr. Ross not only practiced medicine, she fought for women's rights in the medical establishment as well. In 1863, she applied for admission to the Milwaukee County Medical Society, but the distinguished doctors in the society were so concerned that admission of a woman doctor would damage their elite status, they delayed action on her petition. The doctors could not actually refuse Ross admission because her character, credentials, and competence were impeccable. But they hoped that a delay would convince the "ladylike" Dr. Ross to quietly withdraw her application. The Society's members were wrong about the "ladylike" Dr. Ross. She continued to apply for membership year after year — for six years — until the Society reluctantly voted her admission in 1869.[46]

Betsy Thunder

There was a time, not so long ago, when Wisconsin Indians were free to gather whatever roots and plants they needed to make their medicines. In those days, too, Indians had the time to learn the techniques and the ceremonies for collecting these medicines, preparing them and administering them. Betsy Thunder lived during that time and practiced tribal medicine in Jackson County, Wisconsin from the 1850's until 1912.[47]

A member of the Winnebago Sky Clan, Betsy Thunder was a descendant of the Decorahs and the sister of Grey Eagle. She married young and well to Whirling Thunder, an older man of great prestige in the tribe. Because of his age, Whirling Thunder knew he would not be able to pass on his medicine to his children so he taught all he knew to his young bride and entrusted her to pass it on to the next generation.

Betsy Thunder was a careful student. In her lifetime she came to be known and trusted in the Winnebago and white communities as a medical practitioner of great skill. She spoke very little English but did not feel it was important for her to talk to her patients in order to cure them. What was important was to conduct the proper ceremonies in collecting, preparing and administering the medicines. There was a song for every root and a history to be spoken during every treatment. It took years of work and study for Betsy Thunder to learn these ceremonies. They are not written down; each one must be memorized.

Like all Winnebago healers, Betsy Thunder received 'gifts' for her medical services. These gifts were not a payment; they were a symbol of the patient's willingness or desire to be cured. Medicines were thought to be useless if the patient was not willing to offer something valuable — like clothes, food or blankets — for the medicine.

Betsy Thunder treated countless numbers of people — both whites and Winnebagoes — in the area around Shamrock, near Manchester Township in Jackson County. One of her patients was Mary Mills, the daughter of John Mills, a wealthy banker and lumberman in the area. The child had been sick for days and several white doctors had come and gone, having exhausted their skills and knowledge. Finally, Mills sent for Betsy Thunder. She was able to cure the child in a few days with her assortment of 'roots, herbs, gums, barks, and berries.' John Mills never forgot Betsy Thunder's service. He kept a room for her in his large house where she stayed when she went to town and he gave her the lumber to build a small cabin on the 20 acres she owned near Shamrock. The people of Shamrock built the cabin in appreciation of Thunder's years of healing among them.

The Wisconsin Winnebagoes were "removed" to Nebraska by order of the U.S. government in the early 1900's. Some went to Nebraska and stayed there. Many more went and came back. Betsy Thunder never went. She and many of her people hid out in the hills of Jackson County, living as they had always lived; by hunting, gardening and berrypicking. Thunder never left Wisconsin, explains her granddaughter, because "we were put here in Wisconsin . . . It isn't because the country here is beautiful; it's because our 'god' put us in Wisconsin and this is where we are supposed to be."

Betsy Thunder lived out her entire life in Wisconsin on the sandy soil the government finally gave to the Wisconsin 'remnant' or 'strays' as they called the remaining Winnebagoes. She never converted to Christianity or moved near the Black River Falls Indian Mission that was established in the 1870's. Like all traditional Winnebagoes who belonged to the medicine lodge, Thunder thought that Christian converts were "lost." She taught her children and her grandchildren that "you have to keep believing in what the old people believed in" and she died before the post-World War I "re-education" of Native Americans began.

Rhoda Lavinia Goodell

Rhoda Lavinia Goodell of Janesville was the first woman to apply for admission to the bar of the Wisconsin State Supreme Court. She had been practicing law in Janesville for a year and a half, as a member of the Rock County Circuit Court, when she appeared before Chief Justice Ryan in Madison on December 14, 1875. Goodell prepared the argument on her own behalf but had to enlist a male colleague to present it in court.[48]

Goodell was 36 years old and a woman of considerable experience and stature when she came before the Wisconsin Supreme Court. Born in New York and a graduate of Ladies' Seminary in Brooklyn Heights, she had edited an abolition newspaper with her father for five years, had taught school for three years, and had worked as an editor at *Harper's Bazaar* in New York for four years. She moved to Janesville with her aged parents in 1871 where she took up the study of law in the office of Jackson and Norcross. After three years of study she was found competent to practice law in Rock County. The respect and success which she knew as a lawyer in Janesville encouraged her to apply for admission to the State Supreme Court.[49]

In her argument for admission Goodell contended that there was no stated legislative restriction *against* women practicing law before the Supreme Court, that the use of the male gender in legislative codes was commonly understood to refer to females as well as males, and that the admission of women to the U.W. law school implied their admission to the bar of the Supreme Court. Goodell argued further that to exclude women from the full practice of law served to leave one half of the human race unrepresented in courts of justice and prevented the "free and wholesome competition of the best existing legal talent in the community." Goodell concluded that "a great injustice is done to one-half the community by shutting them out arbitrarily from an honorable and remunerative field of industry, for which many of them have both taste and ability."[50]

Goodell's case fell on deaf ears. Chief Justice Ryan disallowed all of her arguments and denied her application. In his decision Ryan called Goodell "a lady whose character raises no personal objection; something perhaps not always to be found in women who deny the ways of their sex for the ways of ours."[51] According to Ryan, the legislature had never intended to "emasculate the constitution" by considering females the same as males. This, he claimed, would be "a confusion of the functions of the sexes . . . a sweeping revolution of the social order."[52]

"We cannot but think the common law wise in excluding women from the profession of law," wrote Justice Ryan. "The profession . . . exacts the devotion of life. The law of nature destines and qualifies the female sex for the bearing and nurture of the children of our race and for the custody of the homes of the world . . .And all life-long callings of women inconsistent with these sacred duties of their sex, as is the profession of law, are departures from the order of nature; and, when voluntary, treason against it . . .It is public policy to provide for the sex . . .and not to tempt women from the proper duties of their sex by opening to them duties peculiar to ours.

"The peculiar qualities of womanhood, its gentle graces, its quick sensibility, its tender susceptibility, its purity, its delicacy, its emotional impulses, its subordination of hard reason to sympathetic feeling, are surely not qualifications for forensic strife. Womanhood is moulded for gentler and better things . . .Discussions are habitually necessary in courts of justice which are unfit for female ears. The habitual presence of women at these would tend to relax the public sense of decency and propriety."[53]

Goodell returned to Janesville and continued to practice law in Rock County. On March 8, 1877 the Wisconsin legislature overruled Chief Justice Ryan's decision with an act providing that "no person shall be denied a license (to practice law in the courts of the state) on account of sex." As a result of this new law, Rhoda Goodell was admitted to the bar of the Wisconsin State Supreme Court in June, 1879. She died less than a year later.[54]

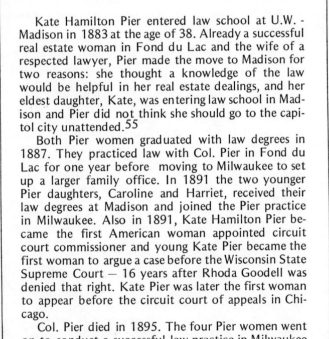

Kate Hamilton Pier entered law school at U.W. - Madison in 1883 at the age of 38. Already a successful real estate woman in Fond du Lac and the wife of a respected lawyer, Pier made the move to Madison for two reasons: she thought a knowledge of the law would be helpful in her real estate dealings, and her eldest daughter, Kate, was entering law school in Madison and Pier did not think she should go to the capitol city unattended.[55]

Both Pier women graduated with law degrees in 1887. They practiced law with Col. Pier in Fond du Lac for one year before moving to Milwaukee to set up a larger family office. In 1891 the two younger Pier daughters, Caroline and Harriet, received their law degrees at Madison and joined the Pier practice in Milwaukee. Also in 1891, Kate Hamilton Pier became the first American woman appointed circuit court commissioner and young Kate Pier became the first woman to argue a case before the Wisconsin State Supreme Court — 16 years after Rhoda Goodell was denied that right. Kate Pier was later the first woman to appear before the circuit court of appeals in Chicago.

Col. Pier died in 1895. The four Pier women went on to conduct a successful law practice in Milwaukee and manage their sizeable land holdings in northern Wisconsin. They were also instrumental in the formation of a separate organization for Wisconsin's women lawyers and were active members of the National Women Lawyers Association.

Wisconsin Women Begin
the Fight for Suffrage

"The holy, loving influence of the wife and mother, her making the house, the family, the earthly paradise of man, are the only powerful moral and social reformers, and that dignity is the highest on earth, and high over the ballot box."

—*"A German Democrat"*
Letter to the Milwaukee
Sentinel, *1869.*[56]

"I confess I never before found myself in the midst of such a conservative society. To affirm one's faith in woman suffrage is about as much as one's social position is worth, and for a woman to actually declare that she desires to go to the polls and vote, produces an effect not unlike that which might be produced should she express the desire to commit burglary or arson."

—*Woman Immigrant to Racine*
Letter to The Woman's Journal, *1873.*[57]

❖❖❖❖❖❖❖❖❖❖❖❖❖❖❖❖❖❖❖❖❖❖❖❖❖❖❖❖❖

On September 7, 1882 thirty-five men and women met in Madison to organize the Wisconsin Woman's Suffrage Association. Two previous attempts at forming a statewide organization had failed. This one would succeed and endure for 38 years — the time it took for Wisconsin women to win the vote.[58]

❖❖❖❖❖❖❖❖❖❖❖❖❖❖❖❖❖❖❖❖❖❖❖❖❖❖❖❖❖

"So far the agitators have made little progress in convincing their own sex. The great majority of women seem to be content with exclusion from the responsibilities of government and manifest no absorbing ambition to fill the offices."

—The Racine Journal, *1882*[59]

"Men say women don't want the vote. That is none of their business. If they have deprived us of a privilege which is ours by right . . .it is their business to right the wrong done whether we ask it or not."

—*Nancy Comstock, 1885*
speech in Milwaukee.[60]

Pauline Jacobus

In 1880, Pauline Jacobus was a wealthy society matron living in Chicago and teaching the "genteel art of China-painting" in her home. One day she saw an exhibit of clay work by Sarah Bernhardt and decided that she must try to work with that medium. Jacobus went off to the Rockwood Potteries in Cincinnati to learn the entire process — from the throwing and molding of pots to the operation of the kilns — and returned to Chicago to establish the city's first studio for producing and decorating art pottery.[61]

Between 1883 and 1888, Pauline Jacobus enjoyed great success. She was selling her work at Tiffany's in New York, Kimball's in Boston and Marshall Field's in Chicago. And she was out-growing her home workshop. The time had come to move and to find an independent source of raw materials. Jacobus went into partnership with her husband, Oscar. Together they located a rich bed of clay in Edgerton, Wisconsin and signed a contract with Bell Telephone to make porous cups for batteries. The money from this contract, plus the money raised through subscriptions allowed the Jacobus' to finance the Pauline Pottery Company in Edgerton.

Pauline Jacobus employed thirteen women to decorate pottery at the plant in Edgerton. She was in charge of every phase of the pottery operation and could substitute for any of her workers if necessary. Meanwhile, Oscar Jacobus supervised twenty men in making the Bell Company's porous cups. The Pauline Pottery Company prospered for five years, until 1893, when Mr. Jacobus died. Then, with the loss of the Bell Company contract, the pottery company passed out of Mrs. Jacobus' hands. She retired to her brick mansion on the edge of town where for eight years she taught leather tooling, stencilling, and clay modeling. Students paid $20 for four weeks of classes and $7 more if they wished room and board.

Jacobus was not to be held back by circumstance, however. She saved her money and in 1901 she bought back her still-standing kiln and was given the remaining piles of clay. "Thereupon," writes historian Bertha K. Whyte, "she performed one of the outstanding feats of her life. With a common but intelligent bricklayer she managed to get the kiln taken apart, brick by brick, with locations and dimensions carefully recorded in her notebook . . .and then had the kiln rebuilt in a shed behind her house." Whyte quotes Jacobus on her feelings about that rebuilt kiln:

"I don't suppose that any potter ever watched with more anxiety the output of that first burning. It was one thing to have theories of how a kiln should be built and quite another to feel solely responsible for the way in which it had been built . . .I was in a fever of excitement until I had made sure that everything was all right — that my kiln could do as good work as the old one which had been built by a professional builder . . .You see it meant a complete shattering of all hopes I had entertained for years of sometime owning a kiln again if things had not turned out well."[62]

For the next eight years Jacobus turned out remarkable quantities of platters, bowls, vases, tobacco jars and rose petal jars, doing all the clay work herself and using students to assist with the painting. Unlike other clay works which were using molds at this time, Pauline Pottery pieces were all turned out on a wheel and decorated by hand. According to Pauline Grant of Edgerton, little of Jacobus' work exists today because her skill lay more in design and painting than in ceramics.[63] Nonetheless, there are enough pieces remaining in collections, such as the Middleton Collection at the Wisconsin State Historical Society, to suggest that "Mrs. Jacobus was willing to try her hand at anything."[64] Her wide-ranging designs and styles are distinctive for their muted tones of yellow, cream, green and blue.

Jacobus closed her shop in 1909 at the age of 69. Some years later she moved to the Masonic Home in Dousman where she died in 1930. "By then," says Grant, "the memory of Pauline Pottery was so faint that no Wisconsin or Chicago paper noted her death."[65]

The Woman's Club of Milwaukee had been meeting in members' homes and public rooms for ten years but as the membership was growing, so grew the problem of finding a suitable meeting place. Finally, in 1886, the women decided to form a stock company for the purpose of building their own meeting place. One thousand shares at $25 each were sold to members of the Milwaukee Woman's Club and "carefully selected (women) friends." By October of 1886 the women were ready to sign the articles of association for the world's first stock company to be created solely by and for women. The company bought a plot of land at Cass and Biddle Streets for $9,400; designed and built a substantial two-story structure complete with meeting rooms, a reception hall, a library and dressing rooms, for $14,000; and was ready to open in December, 1888. The building was called the Milwaukee Atheneum and was, for years, the center of Milwaukee's social life. By renting space to the Woman's Club for $500 a year and providing rooms at reasonable rates to many community organizations for meetings, banquets, balls, and receptions, the Atheneum Corporation performed a service for the city of Milwaukee and involved many women in a successful business venture.[66]

Helen Bruneau VanVechten

"I haven't many theories about my work except . . . that to make good books one must do honest, careful work . . . a handmade book is like handmade underclothing or handmade anything else. It has its individuality and it represents human skill and intelligence."[67]

When Helen Bruneau VanVechten spoke those words to a Milwaukee newspaper reporter, she was standing in her print shop — the Philosopher Press — in Wausau, Wisconsin. The year was 1889 and VanVechten had been working with her husband, Phillip, and their partner, William Ellis, for about three years. The Philosopher Press was one of the earliest private presses to spring up in this country during the 'private press movement' of the late 19th and early 20th centuries. The movement and its trio of Wausau followers believed that bookmaking

had been corrupted by the use of machinery and the commercial desire for speed and efficiency. The 'Philosophers' devoted themselves to resisting technology and restoring a sense of art and craftsmanship to the business of bookmaking.[68]

Neither VanVechten nor the Philosopher Press have been accorded a place in history; but in her day VanVechten was known and respected by rare book collectors all over the world. The Press' reputation far exceeded the size of its operation because of the quality of its books and because of the lifestyle Helen VanVechten and her colleagues carved out in the northern Wisconsin woods. From the time of its founding in 1896, the Philosopher Press served as a meeting place for intellectuals and would-be authors from all over the state. According to several accounts, this coterie that called themselves 'the Philosophers' would sit around the shop's sheet iron stove "in an atmosphere blue with smoke," to talk and laugh and argue about books, politics, art, printing and philosophy. "It's the sort of life," sighed one reporter, "that most people go to their graves still dreaming about — a hardworking, earnest, joyous bohemia where the small conventions give way before the great things of life."[69]

Helen VanVechten and William Ellis did their work in this "joyous bohemia," (Phillip VanVechten went to work in the office of a Wausau lumber company in 1897 but remained a financial and spiritual partner and a stove-side 'Philosopher'). Here they printed limited editions of such classics as "The Rubaiyat of Omar Khayham," and R.W. Emerson's "Self-Reliance," in addition to putting out a monthly 'chap-book' called the "The Philosopher" which carried artistic reviews, social comment, and art work.

The Philosopher Press did not design its own type or mix its own ink, but thanks to Helen VanVechten it did become notable for one very significant printing achievement: its perfect registry. It was thought impossible at that time to get a perfect registry on the deckle-edged paper used by private presses. The handmade paper was not cut on the square and hand printers could not make the printing on the back side of a sheet line up with the printing on the front side. Unaware that the world's experts considered this an insurmountable problem, Helen VanVechten determined how to solve it. She was, at the time, working on a limited edition of Lewis Carroll's "The Hunting of the Snark," and when the red borders that she had designed around each page would not line up, she ordered her skeptical pressman to reverse the paper-feeding process; feeding from left to right on one side and from right to left on the other. Paper had never been fed from right to left and the pressman at first refused. But VanVechten was the boss and she stood firm. The first page they tried came out with a perfect registry, as did the next and the next.[70]

VanVechten had revolutionized the appearance of hand-printed books and had, in the process, made her own name in the world of hand printing. From that time on, she signed all the books she printed, indicating that she had printed every page herself, putting the sheets through the press, attending to the ink distribution and insuring that every letter was flawless. Books printed by Helen Bruneau VanVechten were reviewed in the state and national press and sought by collectors all over the world. Only two years after printing her edition of "The Hunting of the Snark," the book's value had climbed to four times its original price.[71]

This was quite a success story for a young woman who had grown up in Wausau, attended Milwaukee College (later Milwaukee-Downer) and married Phillip VanVechten, the son of a well-to-do Milwaukee family. Helen Bruneau had returned to Wausau with her husband with the rather unambitious idea of becoming the bookkeeper in his new printing venture with William Ellis. But she was, reportedly, a brilliant conversationalist and an interested student of printing. Before long, she had a permanent place in the Philosophers' circle and had replaced her husband as Ellis' co-worker.

We know from her correspondence that VanVechten was a respected friend and colleague among hand printers all over the country. And we know from her niece, Mrs. A.M. Evans of Wausau, that she had "quite a library . . . She was interested in East Indian religions and had a fine collection of books on metaphysics."[72] She was also president of the 'Ladies Literary Club' in Wausau and at one time advised a group of children on the printing of their own newspaper. But the center of Helen VanVechten's life was the log cabin that housed the Philosopher Press where she and her partners tried to develop a communal spirit, living, working and creating together according to their creed:

"We believe in the dignity of toil and the joy of work, and that we shall yet win back art to our daily labors."[73]

In 1886, Wisconsin's male voters agreed to a legislative bill giving qualified women the right to vote in "any election pertaining to school matters." On the assumption that *all* elections pertained to school matters, the Reverend Olympia Brown, president of the Wisconsin Woman Suffrage Association, attempted to vote in a municipal election in Racine in 1887. When her ballot was rejected she brought suit against the city. The circuit court agreed with Reverend Brown, but the State Supreme Court reversed the decision on the grounds that the legislature had previously rejected bills giving women full suffrage or even municipal suffrage. The legislative intent was clear, said the Court; women could vote *only* in school elections. A later decision ruled that separate ballot boxes should be provided for women voters, but the legislature did not get around to appropriating funds for such boxes until 1901. From 1901 until 1920 Wisconsin women voters used the separate box and the unequal ballot.[74]

"In the pioneer days of northern Wisconsin, women's organizations were not wholly approved of. It took vision and fortitude, courage and determination for a little band of women to carry out their plan for starting a woman's club in the then-young town of Antigo. But they succeeded in their efforts and the first meeting was held in 1895."
—Eulogy to Ida Wright Albers,
founding member of the Antigo Woman's Club.[75]

Mary Miller Smith began writing her *Memoirs of Long Ago* on her 90th birthday, in 1933. Subtitled, "The Autobiography of a Baptist Preacher's Wife," her 90-page book reveals much of what it has meant to be a church wife in America. When Mary Miller married a preacher in 1865 she not only chose a life of faith and devotion, but a set of obligations and responsibilities as well. For the role of a preacher's wife carries with it an unwritten — but widely accepted — job description. And though the job is seldom recognized and never recompensed, many women like Mary Miller Smith have chosen it for it provided one of the few opportunities for a committed Protestant woman to make a 'career' in the church.

"I had several opportunities for marriage before," wrote Smith, *"but as I look back over the years, I feel very sure that I was guided by Divine Wisdom in rejecting all previous offers until this right opportunity came to me. This event changed my whole life. A new world opened up for me and gave me opportunities for mental and spiritual growth that I never could have had if I had accepted former opportunities for marriage."*[76]

Part III: The Progressive Years

Wisconsin has often been touted as "the birthplace of Progressivism." True or not, there is no denying that Wisconsin was one of the most enthusiastic and influential participants in the reform movement that swept the American states between 1890 and World War I. The mania for social action that accompanied Progressivism touched all classes and all political groups — the rich, the middle class and the poor; the radical, the liberal, and the conservative. Everyone favored 'progress,' 'social betterment,' and 'modernity;' the differences arose when people tried to define these goals.

The Progressive years coincided with a particularly crucial time for American woman. The conditions of modern life had already begun to make her traditional domestic functions obsolete. It was imperative that the 'New Woman' (as the era dubbed her) find something new to do — or that she find a new way of defining what she had always done.

The era's more liberal or radical women found many new things to do and new ways to live. They became politically as well as socially active; they spoke out for woman's right to dictate the course of her own life, they drew themselves together in groups of women, for women, and they dared to enter the executive ranks in business, government and education. Individual women had fought these battles before, but never in such numbers or with such gusto and public pride.

At the same time, there was a movement among conservative progressives to preserve woman's traditional role but imbue it with a modern significance and respect. Conservative women campaigned to show that the difficulties of the modern age made it more important than ever that women stay at home and protect the hearth as a professional homemaker, wife and mother.

Because of the variety of definitions available to the New Woman, the Progressive years produced some of the most interesting and complex women in America's history. And because Wisconsin women were so widely and actively involved in the spirit of this era, they have a particular interest and complexity.

"I believe that taxation without representation is tyranny now as it was in the olden times. This talk about women being represented by the men is all nonsense. I suppose they mean a woman can be represented by her husband, but what are we poor souls without that useful article to do? Besides it is impossible for one individual to think for another in such matters . . . I maintain women should have equal rights."

—Dr. Evelyn Hoehn, Milwaukee
physician. Interview with
The Free Press, 1904.[77]

"The way up the heights of woman's advancement has been long and steep but it has not been dreary. The consciousness of giving the world a forward movement along the path of liberty is the highest reward vouchsafed in human efforts. The greatest men of the century have walked with us. Poets have sung for us, prophets have inspired us with visions of success. Statesmen have made courts and forums ring with eloquence in our behalf . . . Timidity, opposition and indifference have changed into a grand chorus of appeal for woman's equality before the law. Let us then close the 19th century with a convention which shall be a jubilee for our success and the preparation for the 20th century which is to be not man's nor woman's but humanity's."

—Clara Bewick Colby, editorial in The Woman's Tribune *on the eve of the 32nd annual convention of the National-American Woman Suffrage Association in 1900.*[78]

Clara Bewick Colby grew up in southern Wisconsin and was valedictorian in the first class of women to graduate from the University of Wisconsin — Madison in 1869. She taught history and Latin at U.W. for a few years before becoming a professional suffrage worker. Colby traveled all over the country on behalf of woman suffrage and in 1884 founded *The Woman's Tribune,* the official organ of the National-American Woman Suffrage Association. She edited the highly respected *Tribune* until 1909 when lack of funds forced her to cease publication. But she continued to work for suffrage as an organizer and lecturer until her death in 1916 . . . four years before the suffrage was won.[79]

Jane and Ellen Lloyd-Jones

In another place and time, Hillside Home School might have been called an "experimental school." But to its founders, Jane and Ellen Lloyd-Jones, there was nothing experimental about it. It was simply the only sensible way for people — young and old — to live and to learn. Hillside was, from the beginning, a combination home, school, and farm. The three elements were a unity, no single one ever took precedence over another. "To the Aunts," recalled one teacher, "each child, whatever his age, was a person . . .with the rights, privileges and necessities of his own individual make-up. Only one thing was expected of him: that he should live on decent terms with a large and decent family."[80]

Students were not required to attend classes at Hillside, but since teachers integrated their studies with the life of the farm and its residents, newcomers soon found that attending class was the most interesting way to spend the day. Gardening was a central part of life at Hillside. The students had individual gardens and the-satisfaction of knowing that what they produced ¯in their gardens fed the school. Bird-watching and flower-hunting were equally important activities; botany and biology were seldom 'taught' indoors. One teacher recalled her "interview" for a position at Hillside:

"The sisters surprised me by not asking anything about what I knew in the subjects for which they needed a teacher. They wanted to know instead if I liked the country, if children amused me and interested me, if I liked and could take long walks, and if I knew anything about birds and common flowers."[81]

Wisconsin State Historical Society

Jane Lloyd-Jones

There were, at times, as many as 100 residents at Hillside, but there were very few rules. The spirit of cooperation was its own standard and was taught by example, not commandment. This system was aided by the tacit 'assignment' of older students to watch over younger ones.

Wisconsin State Historical Society

Ellen Lloyd-Jones

Before opening the Hillside School in 1887, Jane and Ellen Lloyd-Jones had taught in more conventional surroundings. Jane, the younger and "more vibrant" sister, had been director of kindergarten training schools in St. Paul, Minnesota. Ellen, the "more serene" sister, had been head of the history department at River Falls State Normal School in Wisconsin. When Ellen was 42 and Jane was 39, the two agreed to open a home school for all the Lloyd-Jones nieces and nephews who lived in the family's valley outside Spring Green, Wisconsin. To seal this ambitious plan, the sisters made a compact that they would never marry.[82]

Hillside Home School was built on the site originally settled by Richard and Mary Lloyd-Jones in 1844. They had come to Iowa County from Cardiganshire, Wales and raised ten children on their beautiful valley homestead in Wisconsin. Four of the Lloyd-Jones sons owned farms in that same valley. The fifth, Jenkin, was a well-known Unitarian minister in Chicago and the director of Lincoln Center, a settlement house. Because the family was close-knit and all the children were enrolled at Hillside, the Lloyd-Jones' participated actively in the life of the school. When children from outside the family began coming to Hillside, they soon took to calling the brothers "Uncle Thomas," "Uncle Enos," and even "Uncle Jenk" for he was a frequent visitor. Another frequent visitor was "Cousin Frank," Frank Lloyd Wright, the brash young architect from Chicago who was the son of Ann Lloyd-Jones, Jane and Ellen's older sister.

Few members of the family thought Frank would amount to much — except Aunt Nell and Aunt Jane. In 1903 they asked Frank to design a new main building for Hillside School. Photographs of the building reveal the emerging Wright style: a low structure of wood and limestone with varying pavilions and bays and angles "to keep the boys and girls from growing tired." The Lloyd-Jones uncles were more pleased with this design than they had been in 1888 when Frank designed a new windmill for the school. The design submitted on that occasion was so unusual that the uncles swore it would never stand. But Aunt Nell and Aunt Jane insisted that the design was beautiful and that "if Frank says it will stand, then it will stand." The windmill was built and long after all the aunts and uncles had died and Frank Lloyd Wright had turned Hillside School into "Taliesen East" the windmill stood as a tribute to his aunts' faith in that which was young and experimental.[83]

Hillside School was financially self-sustaining but it went into serious debt when the sisters loaned their brother, James, a large sum of money and James died before repaying it. The Rev. Jenkin Lloyd-Jones took advantage of this situation to buy up a large interest in the school. The Rev. had never trusted two women to run Hillside properly; he now hoped to force his aging sisters to sell out, leaving him to institute his *own* plans for the school. Jane and Ellen held fast against family pressure to relinquish their stock to 'Jenk'. They insisted that the school was rightfully theirs, that it was they who had built and nurtured it and they who should determine its future. "When you have put your life in a large measure into one foolish venture," explained Ellen, ". . .it is pathetic to be *shoved* aside before you have an inclination to lie down."[84]

Rather than lie down, the sisters resisted. Steadfast in their refusal to let Jenk have Hillside but unable to buy him out, they closed the school and moved to Los Angeles. Neither of them lived to see their precious school inherited and used by nephew Frank as a living and learning environment for young architects, one true to the tradition established by Aunt Nell and Aunt Jane.

"Be in a hurry, be impatient, be obstreperous, be disagreeable — you can be if you make an awful effort — and that is the only way you will ever get your rights out of us chivalrous males. It's funny about this chivalry, the way it goes to pieces whenever a woman wants anything a man doesn't want her to have. When a man gets up and gives his chair to a woman he feels that the whole feminine world should be grateful, and when a woman says, 'No thank you, I don't want to sit down,' it knocks to pieces his whole philosophy of life."

— Max Eastman, New York radical, in a 1917 speech to the Wisconsin Woman Suffrage Association convention in Madison.[85]

Before 1921 the guardianship laws in Wisconsin specified that as long as the father was living he had sole legal custody of all minor children. A widow only had custody as long as she remained unmarried.[86]

"A woman who gave her name as Wilson died at Chippewa Falls from a criminal operation performed upon herself. Her parents live near Eau Claire . . .her brother took charge of her remains. The woman was young and pretty and visited every physician in Chippewa Falls to accomplish her object, but without success."

— Newspaper account, April 6, 1893[87]

Lizzie Black Kander

Lizzie Black Kander represents all that was good and all that was perplexing about public women of her day. While her career continually expanded into areas where other women feared to tred, pioneering in the settlement house movement, industrial training and immigrant education; Kander saw her work as a woman in very traditional terms. Conservative Progressive women like Kander believed that it was women's particularly *feminine* instincts that were needed to reform society. By the turn of the century they were arguing that it was every woman's maternal duty to go out and "sweep up" some dirty corner of the city. It was this sense of maternal duty that sparked women like Kander to the kinds of reform activity that we now mistake for feminism. This is not to say that the conservative Progressive women's reform work was not worthwhile or sincere; it is only to point out that women of that ilk were still struggling with their own feelings about their role, their duty and their place. Lizzie Black Kander is a fascinating study of how one very capable woman faced this struggle.[88]

Kander is doubly fascinating because she was a German Reform Jew in Milwaukee at a time when thousands of Russian Orthodox Jews were pouring into that city. Milwaukee's German Jews had already established themselves as respected members of the community. They were, rightly or wrongly, afraid that the influx of uneducated, unemployed Jews from Eastern Europe would unleash a wave of anti-Semitism toward the entire Jewish population. To stave off that wave, Milwaukee's German Jews instituted a raft of social betterment programs designed to 'Americanize' their Russian cousins. Lizzie Black Kander was at the forefront of this movement to reeducate the Russians and as a leader she served two clients: the Jewish women of Milwaukee society and the Russian Jews of the Milwaukee slum. According to Ann Shirley Waligorski who wrote a masters' thesis on Kander, "For women like herself who were middle-class, overeducated and without a meaningful job in a rapidly changing environment, social work served as a safety valve; it was as much a need of well-off women in order that they might develop a sense of self-worth as a response to the degradation of the slums."

Kander got involved with social welfare work in 1878. The young bride of a clothing salesman, she joined the Ladies' Relief Sewing Society and was appointed to the South Side Truancy Committee. The rapid influx of Russians in the 1880's and the depression of 1890 convinced Kander that traditional forms of charity, like the sewing society, were no longer adequate. Unlike many welfare workers of her day, Kander recognized that immigrant poverty was a social, *not* a moral, problem. As early as 1896 she told the Ladies Relief Society that "the immigrant poor are a direct result of tyranny and oppression, of the persecutions

that have been heaped upon them from generation to generation to generation . . .(they) are disheartened and discouraged having been robbed of all their worldly possessions, driven from their homes and forced in their advanced years and with large families to start life anew — in a strange land — amidst new people, who cannot even understand their language."

Kander's analysis of the problem was unusual but her solution was not. Like most reformers of her day, she firmly believed that the best thing she could do for these people was to Americanize them, and if not them, then their children. Working through the Ladies' Relief Society, Kander convinced her friends that a more permanent institution was needed to convert Russian Jews into American Jews. The decision was made to open a Jewish mission because Russian Jews did not trust Christian missions and would not attend classes there. The Milwaukee Jewish mission began in 1896 in the small back room of a downtown temple, but by 1900 it had a separate building and a new name: The Settlement. As director of the Mission/Settlement, Kander organized public and financial support from community leaders and businessmen — a task she was particularly skilled at — and attracted a corps of volunteer teachers and eager students. The program was constantly expanding, necessitating moves to larger quarters in 1904, 1912, and 1931.

From its earliest years the Settlement had classes for all ages and interests — sewing, reading, woodworking, English, dancing, manual training and, of course, cooking. Kander's cooking classes, many of which she taught herself, became famous for two reasons. They were the only cooking classes outside New York City that observed strict Kosher law; and they were the first and only Settlement house cooking classes to publish a commercially successful cookbook. *The Settlement Cookbook*, subtitled "The Way to a Man's Heart," was first published in 1901. It is still published and is still used in kitchens all over the United States. Kander designed it as a way to share Settlement women's ethnic recipes while at the same time imparting tips about consumer short-cuts and American cooking. The idea was good and the recipes were excellent; the 200-page book was an immediate sell-out and continued to sell out year after year. In time, the book became the Settlement's main source of fiscal support.

That something so traditionally female as a cookbook should have become the financial support of the Jewish Settlement epitomizes Lizzie Black Kander's career. Here was a strong, capable administrator, a person of considerable power and presence, a crusader, a reformer . . .and a woman whose single purpose was to maintain the traditional American family. She sought to train foreign women for their roles as American wives and mothers because she believed that women were the pillar of the family and the family was the pillar of democracy.

A prime example of the Kander philosophy was her work as a member of the Milwaukee Board of Education from 1908 to 1919, during which time she was the main force behind the establishment of the Girls' Trade School. Kander argued that training girls in a skill would cultivate thrift, diligence and industry and would keep them from prostitution. Second, she said, training women to perform the sewing, baking and food processing functions that were being done in factories would serve to restore to women their traditional repsonsibilities. But third and most important, argued Kander, women who were trained in scientific cooking and sewing would create clean, healthy, happy American homes suited for the modern world. Although industrial training would fit young women to get jobs in the business world, it was their later careers as wives and mothers that most concerned Kander. "Since the desire to become a happy homemaker is innate in every women," explained Kander, "it seems only right and just to give her the opportunity to be trained to become what she was intended for."

Rachel Szold Jastrow was, among many things, the founder of the Madison chapter of Hadassah, the Zionist women's organization. Jastrow came to Madison in 1888 as a bride of 21, married to one of U.W.'s first experimental psychologists, Joseph Jastrow. In a few years, she grew from a shy young girl into one of the city's most forceful women. Active in the Woman's Club, the Woman's Peace Party, the Woman's International League for Peace and Freedom, and the Wisconsin Woman Suffrage Association, she was instrumental in the founding of Temple Beth El and Madison General Hospital.[89] Jastrow's sister, Henrietta Szold, was one of the founders of the original chapter of Hadassah in New York City. Encouraged by her sister's efforts, Jastrow convened Madison's first Hadassah meeting in 1915. The small group of 12 women began by hemming diapers for babies in Jerusalem, but it grew in time into an effective organization for education and philanthropy on behalf of Jewish people everywhere.[90]

Among the 550 women graduates from Lawrence, previous to the class of 1913, 220 have taught school, 36 have married ministers, 129 have become homemakers, and 85 have become actively engaged in the business or professional world.

Of the 30 professionals, six are editors and assistant editors, five preachers, five artists, five professors, one teacher of book binding, three nurses, three superintendents of schools and two doctors . . .Business opportunities have called 15 . . .Eight are sales ladies and head clerks, six stenographers, and one contractor-builder.

Nine are actively engaged in some form of library work. Seven are authors. . .Foreign and home missionary work has interested 13 . . . Running a ranch, representing Uncle Sam as a postmaster, teaching the young Honoluluians sanitation by directing a portion of the Pure Foods Department, farming and lecturing on the lyceum platform . . .art metal work, the opera and juvenile courts are the vocations of 11 former Lawrence coeds.

—*The Lawrentian*, May 31, 1916[91]

"I believe that the whole anti-coeducation movement rests upon the present-day competition of women with men. It has gone so far that men are driven out even of machine shops by women . . .The great crucial fact of today, for the future of the race lies in it, is that woman deprives man not merely of his former opportunities for employment, but of herself . . .The college girl is visibly preparing herself to compete with the college boy and to live without him . . .Misogyny is no mere college phenomenon. It is world-wide and woman is hated solely because more and more man is prevented from loving her."

—"The Movement Against Coeducation at the University of Wisconsin," by Wardon A. Curtis, August, 1908.[92]

C.L. Sholes of Milwaukee was the inventor of the typewriter. He was once asked if he didn't think his invention had done a "wonderful thing for the world." He replied, "I don't know about the world, but I do feel that I have done something for the women who have always had to work so hard. It will enable them more easily to earn a living."93

Sholes died in 1890 before the first typewriter was introduced into the State Capitol at Madison. Fifty years later more than 2,000 typewriters were in active state service. Over 90 per cent of them were operated by women.94

Women Employees at the State Capitol

"No one seems to know just how long it is since a woman's name first went down on the state capitol payroll . . .The blue books throw little light on the subject for the very old ones do not mention any women employees at all and the later ones do not take cognizance of all the work that is done by women in the capitol. The number has materially increased, however, in the last few years under the regime of the woman stenographer and typewriter, while more women are also holding clerkships of greater or less importance in the various state departments.

"One of the women who have been in office the longest is Miss Mary W. Priestly, of Mineral Point, who for nine years has been in the office of the adjutant general. Her technical name is 'Clerk of the National Guard Division' but in her long tenure in office she has come to have an intimate acquaintance with the working of the entire office. When the Spanish-American war broke out she was kept busy with the transfer of guardsmen to the regular army and since the close of the war the reorganization of the National Guard has made her a great deal of extra work, every bit of which, however, she says she thoroughly enjoys because it is the next best thing to being a soldier and that is what she most wanted to be when she was a child and did not understand the fine discriminations of the grown-up world."

—*The Milwaukee Sentinel,*
April 1, 190595

Mary Derenzo was an immigrant to Madison, Wisconsin from Rome, Italy. Before the fire of 1900 destroyed the state capitol in Madison, Derenzo was employed as one of the capitol housekeepers. With the capitol a burnt rubble, Derenzo was out of a job. That same year, she was widowed and left with five small children to support and no pension. She went to Governor Robert LaFollette, Sr. and told him her plight. He told her to go to work on the capitol construction crew and until the new capitol was built Mary Derenzo was employed pushing a wheelbarrow.96

Lutie Stearns

When the Wisconsin Free Library Commission began its work in 1895, Wisconsin had only 35 free public libraries. There were 1,700,000 people in the state by then; almost 80 per cent of them living in rural areas and not a few of them in the isolated lumber country of the north and northwest. Most of this population had no access to books. The woman who brought books to the people of Wisconsin was Lutie Stearns. Between 1895 and 1914 Stearns traveled thousands of miles by stage, sleigh, buggy, wagon, passenger coach and caboose, wore out five fur coats in the process, established over 150 free public libraries, and 1,400 traveling libraries, and enabled tens of thousands of Wisconsin residents to become informed and involved in the modern world.[97]

Stearns was not trained as a librarian but she understood libraries' potential as a force for education and social action among the people. Her greatest contribution as library organizer was in convincing people that they wanted libraries. Hers was a 20-year crusade, during which time she visited and revisited towns, gave lectures, conducted surveys, recommended better library procedures, assisted communities in obtaining Carnegie grants, advised in book selection, trained librarians and dealt with local town councils. Between 1896 and 1903 alone, she visited and revisited 130 towns. In one six-month period

Wisconsin State Historical Society

she gave 56 lectures. A sample week's itinerary showed that she covered approximately 550 miles in northern and central Wisconsin. She had a staff of one: Lutie Stearns.[98]

Stearns' first job in a community was to convince one person to take the responsibility for the traveling library. Stearns then sent that person a package of books — 30 for 'isolated hamlets,' 35 for regular stations, and 100 for small public libraries. The package stayed in each locale for six months before being sent on to the next. In time, Stearns might assist a community in building a permanent library and advise in its selection of books. It was her responsibility to develop interesting collections for the traveling libraries as well as developing specialized 'study libraries' which groups could order if they wished to pursue a specific topic. When Stearns realized how much of her client population was foreign born she also instituted foreign language collections.

The purpose in all her activity was to reach people who were isolated, to provide entertainment, information and relaxation for the thousands of Wisconsin citizens who had no contact with the outside world for months at a time. Stearns recalled meeting one woman in the northern woods where "the loneliness was so great, the isolation so unendurable, the enforced idleness of the winter months so hideous, that she unpicked and remade, unpicked and remade her scanty wardrobe, unraveled and reknit, unraveled and reknit her stockings so as to keep the balance of her mind."[99]

As the years went by people came to know and use the traveling library service, writing in regularly for books, creating their own courses of study, and thus continuing their education in the wilderness. "I am a mother of eleven children, all under the age of 21," wrote one farm woman. "We all enjoy reading. If you haven't the books I've listed, please pick out some others. I would like some that would help me in keeping up with the questions of the day."[100]

As a Progressive and as one who had been out in the hinterlands for years, Stearns had great faith in the power of the people and great hopes for their political awakening. She was gratified with her library work but felt politically constrained by her role as a public employee. By 1914 she knew it was time to strike out on her own, to campaign for more than one cause and to make her own personal political statement. Between 1914 and her death in 1943 she was a free-lance lecturer and a columnist for the *Milwaukee Sentinel.* During this time she campaigned for woman suffrage, world peace, temperance, better working conditions for women, educational reform, and a host of other Progressive issues. While engaged in all these activities, Stearns was battling skin cancer and an internal disorder that required the removal of half her stomach. And for all her success as a lecturer, she had a life-long stammer and a terrible fear of speaking in front of people.[101]

Lutie Stearns' interests and ideas were so broad that any summary is inadequate. But we can get a flavor of her Progressivism and her personality by listening to what she said . . .

On Her Politics: *"I am numbered among the radicals. I am not a liberal, as I agree with Heywood Broun that 'a liberal is a man who has just left the room when the fighting begins!"*[102]

On Woman Suffrage: *"The results of the enfranchisement of women have been one of the greatest disappointments of my life . . . Our women have never realized their power . . . The able women ofttimes are willing to stick stamps on envelopes in political campaigns without demanding recognition in the way of office when worthy."*[103]

On Human Rights: *"No human being has the right to domination over the life of another soul even though employed by or related to him. Such domination is a form of human slavery . . . The word 'obey' in the marriage ritual was, of course, inserted by the men framers of the rite as a survival of the old-time regard for women as sexual vassals to men. The right of every woman to her own body should be sacred."*[104]

On War: *"One of the appalling things about the present war is its astronomical cost, much of which is expended on powder which is blown to hell, while thousands of young men who should have the right to live die as the result of expensive explosives."*[105]

On Jane Addams: *"She would have been a wonderful President of these United States and it is my everlasting regret that the women of this country did not rise up against narrow partisan politics and demand that she be our leader."*[106]

On Her Health: *"Throughout my long experience with physical ills I have found one advantage and consolation in being homely: one can only look a little better or a little worse than usual."*[107]

VOTES FOR WOMEN

> Mother mends my socks and shirts,
> Mother mends my coat,
> Mebbe she could mend some laws,
> If she had the vote.
> —Suffrage Banner,
> Campaign of 1912[108]

The Wisconsin Woman Suffrage Association, like all other state suffrage associations, worked at the state and local level to educate, agitate and demonstrate for woman suffrage. The state organization *hoped* for a federal amendment granting woman suffrage nationally and focused much of its effort at developing statewide support for such an amendment. But the Wisconsin group also worked for a state suffrage law allowing women to vote in all state and local elections.

The Wisconsin Woman Suffrage Association introduced woman suffrage bills in the Wisconsin Assembly at almost every session between 1882 and 1912. The suffragists thought a victory was imminent when, in 1912, the Wisconsin legislature agreed to a statewide referendum on the issue. The campaign of 1912 enlisted thousands of new workers in the suffrage cause. Many of these women thought the Wisconsin Woman Suffrage Association was too conservative in its campaign style. They created a second state organization, the Political Equality League.[109]

"The Political Equality League embarked on a campaign deliberately patterned on the spectacular appeal of the circus sideshow. As in the circus, the parade played its part . . .In the larger cities smart-stepping brass bands and lines of marching women attracted crowds . . .The suffragists did not peddle pink lemonade, but they did have vendors who sold cold buttermilk along the line of march, while others passed out

Wisconsin State Historical Society
Strategy Meeting: The Political Equality League, 1912

literature and sold large yellow balloons emblazoned with "Votes for Women" in red letters . . .When Buffalo Bill's Wild West Circus came to Green Bay, they persuaded the famous scout to carry a suffragist banner as he paraded down the main street. Throughout the summer and fall of 1912, almost anywhere a crowd gathered the suffrage speakers were on hand. A group of them on the launch "Mary E." cruised 50 miles up the Wolf River and stopped to speak for equal rights at every available landing. In the vaudeville theaters captive audiences viewed a two-reel 'photoplay' entitled "Votes for Women," and music lovers at the night band concerts in the park were entertained by suffragists who played instrumental solos and pleaded their cause. They spoke before labor union conventions, businessmen's clubs, and county fairs. . .but it was by automobile tours that they reached the voters in Wisconsin's many hamlets and at the crossroads."110

The woman suffrage referendum of 1912 was rejected by the men of Wisconsin, 227,054 to 135,736. Two months after their defeat the suffragists of the state regrouped under one rejuvenated organization: The Wisconsin Woman Suffrage Association. The Association continued to introduce state suffrage bills, to build its membership, and to publish its newspaper, *The Wisconsin Citizen.*111

The Wisconsin Citizen

Suffrage School

"The W.W.S.A. is sponsoring a suffrage school at the Madison Free Library from June 19 to June 22, 1914. Speakers will include:

Rev. Olympia Brown — The History of Woman Suffrage

Zona Gale — Civics and Politics

Harriet Grim — Public Speaking for Suffrage

Mrs. E.S. Jordan — Financing a County Campaign

Ada L. James — Practical Politics for Women"
—June, 1914

Businesswomen's Club

"Miss Melissa Brown, one of the prominent business women of Madison and owner of the College Book Store on State Street has been the leader in organizing a Business Woman's Suffrage club with an initial membership of 101. Any woman who earns her own living is eligible as a member of this club. The organization expects to take up the study of civics and a speech on some question of public interest will be given at every one of the monthly meetings. Much enthusiasm has been manifested."
—November, 1914

"The W.C.T.U. of Juda, Wisconsin makes suffrage the subject of every third meeting."

—March, 1915

General Federation of Women's Clubs
Endorses Woman Suffrage at Biennial Meeting

"The woman's club has been headed straight for the ballot box ever since its inception. Its members did not know where they were going, or they never would have started since they were very conservative and 'woman's rights' had a terrifying sound. Self-culture was their only aim in the early days, but they were drawn gradually into the larger interests of community and state. Imperceptibly, one by one, they came to the realization that it was only through the ballot that they could do most effective work for the home and for society . . . .

"The action of the Biennial meeting is of great importance to the suffrage movement, but it is of even more importance to the clubs themselves. Many of the ablest club women have been developing the opinion that the clubs were afraid of any question which was really timely and vital . . . These Doubting Thomases will now return joyously to the fold."
—July, 1914

Suffrage Marathon

"Mrs. Robert LaFollette, suffragist, and Miss Lucy Price, anti-suffragist, are going to debate sixty-five times on sixty-five successive days beginning July 1. They will tour the midwest under the management of the Coit-Aber Chautauqua Co. And yet there are those who say women should not vote because they have less endurance than men."
—July, 1914

Suffrage campaign on the road in Sister Bay, 1912

Julia Grace Wales

The outbreak of total war in Europe hit like a torpedo at the heart of Progressive America. This country had spent the past 30 years convincing itself that pain and suffering and human degradation could be overcome with the scientific spirit and rational discourse. Julia Grace Wales was a child of this Progressive vision and when the war broke out in Europe she responded with shocked disbelief and moral outrage.

Wales was 33 years old when the war began, a Shakespearian scholar, an English instructor at U.W.-Madison and a dedicated Christian. The war violated everything she believed in: order, compassion, rationality, and social progress. She simply refused to accept it — and she was not alone. The peace movement of 1914-1917 drew heavily from the ranks of American's intellectuals, Christians and Progressives. Never an underground movement, it included some of the biggest names in the country: Jane Addams, of settlement house and suffrage fame; Hamilton Holt, editor of *The Independent;* and David Starr Jordan, prominent scientist and chancellor of Stanford University. Wisconsin peace activists included President Charles VanHise of the University of Wisconsin-Madison; Louise Phelps Kellogg, senior research associate at the Wisconsin State Historical Society; Mary Bradford, Superintendent of Schools in Kenosha; and, of course, Sentor Robert LaFollette, Jr.[112]

Under ordinary circumstances, Julia Grace Wales would have been a little fish in such a big pond, but these were not ordinary circumstances. From August until December of 1914, Wales was driven by her outrage at the war. "The pity and horror of it seized upon her," recalled Louise Kellogg. "She thought night and day of some possible exit from the entanglement in which she felt the world had been unwittingly plunged."[113]

Wisconsin State Historical Society

Finally, during Christmas vacation of 1914, Wales wrote the first draft of a peace plan, a plan which she believed would end "this irrational war." The essence of the plan was embodied in the title of her 16-page booklet, *Continuous Mediation Without Armistice.* Basically, it proposed that delegates from the 35 neutral nations, including the United States, meet as an International Commission of 'experts' to mediate — with armistice if possible, without it if necessary. On the assumption that nations at war had simply lost their senses, Wales proposed that the Commission function as a "world thinking organ." It would sit as long as the war continued, inviting proposals from all warring nations on ways to bring peace. "Thus, Wales' plan was not in itself an actual plan for peace. . .Rather, it was a proposal for the creation of machinery whereby thoughtful proposals could be formulated and communicated to all belligerents."[114]

Such a proposal was not totally original with Wales, but her idea that the mediation continue regardless of armistice *was* new. This idea, plus the way she presented her plan and the people she presented it to, all combined to make her booklet an instant success and catapulted its author to 'stardom' in the peace movement. Wales originally submitted her book anonymously, thinking that the plan would not be taken seriously if it was known that a woman had designed it. But soon she was in contact with peace activists such as Addams and Holt and her anonymity was lost. Wales could never have imagined the acclaim her plan would receive. Adopted immediately by the Wisconsin Peace Society, it soon came to be called "The Wisconsin Plan." President Wilson received the plan in January, 1915, as did David Starr Jordan who called it "the most forceful and practical thing I have yet seen." The National Peace Conference Meeting in Chicago in February, 1915 adopted the plan as part of its platform and the Wisconsin Legislature endorsed the plan in a resolution sent to President Wilson in March, 1915.

Things must have been moving terribly fast for Julia Wales, who had been living the quiet life of a poet and scholar in Madison for almost ten years. A Canadian by birth and the eldest of three daughters in the family of rural doctor, Wales had attended McGill University in Montreal and received a scholarship to attend Radcliffe for her Master's Degree. She is described by all who wrote about her as a rather shy, quiet person; but the stories of her work in the peace movement and her own correspondence would indicate that when she had something important to say, she had no trouble saying it.[115]

By the spring of 1915, Wales' booklet was being referred to as "the bible of the peace movement," and Wales herself was being called "America's Jean d'Arc." Indeed, her fear that being a woman would affect the plan's reception proved not unfounded. In the press at least, she was continually referred to in a patronizing tone. Ignoring her age and professional status, reporters called her "the little girl with a great idea," dwelling always on her emotional response to the war, the tears in her eyes when she spoke of it.[116]

There is no denying that Wales was emotional about war and peace. She was an admitted spiritualist, more concerned with morality than politics; but she was also an activist and quite able in practical debate. On leave from the University in 1915, she attended the Women's International Peace Congress at the Hague where women gathered together "to prove," said Wales, "that the women of the world are capable of international friendship. . .to coordinate their thinking, and to communicate their aspiration for peace to the neutral and belligerent nations." Wales feared that debate at the Hague conference was being kept safe at the expense of vitality, but strong resolutions were eventually adopted, including a resolution endorsing the Wisconsin Plan.[117]

Wales continued her efforts for peace until America entered the war in 1918. Until then she had been totaly uninterested in arguments about which side was 'right' or 'wrong,' insisting that war for any cause was always the greatest wrong. But with the entry of the U.S., Wales — like the great majority of peace activists — supported the Allied cause.

After the war she continued to teach, aided the WPA during the Depression, and spoke out, briefly, for peace in a 1942 pamphlet entitled *Democracy Needs Education.* She retired as Associate Professor Emeritus from U.W. in 1947 and returned to Canada where she died in 1957. Her great struggle had been futile at the time. But she made a genuine and profound contribution to America's heritage of peace movements.

The Women's International League for Peace and Freedom grew out of the Women's International Peace Congress at the Hague in 1915. A WILPF chapter was formed in Madison, Wisconsin in 1922 after Montana Congresswoman Jeanette Rankin spoke at a large public meeting in the Capitol. The chapter's first major effort was toward abolishing compulsory R.O.T.C at the University of Wisconsin. As a result of WILPF's intense lobbying and well-organized demonstrations at the Capitol, military training was declared optional by the 1923 Wisconsin legislature — a major victory for the newly-formed Madison chapter. Between 1923 and 1926, freshman student enrollment in R.O.T.C. declined from 64% to 18%. When an attempt was made in the 1930's to reinstitute compulsory R.O.T.C., the ever-vigilant women of Madison's WILPF defeated it.[118]

"Women as purveyors of food for their families are making frantic efforts to reduce the cost of living by co-operative buying, by organizing, and by boycotting some articles of food whose price is exorbitantly high. Such action is, as far as we have heard, universally considered quite womanly. At best it will have only small and temporary result. This problem of high price of food is a difficult one. Most of us do not believe that it is brought about wholly or mainly by large demand and small supply. We believe that other forces, especially cold storage institutions, have something to do with it. We believe further that the time is coming. . .when governmental regulation of prices of food. . .will be found absolutely unavoidable. Women without the ballot may try indirectly, weakly and inefficiently to reduce the cost of living. Women with the ballot may strike directly and forcibly at the enemy, by using their ballots to bring about essential governmental regulation. Which course is more womanly?"

—The Wisconsin Citizen, *January, 1917.*[119]

Between 1870 and 1940 almost 50 per cent of Milwaukee's total workforce was employed in manufacturing. In the course of that time period, women took an increasing proportion of the manufacturing jobs. By 1870, about 17 per cent of the persons employed in manufacturing industries were women. By 1910, women held 24 per cent of those jobs and by 1940, over 29 per cent.

Where the heavier industries employed almost no women before 1900, by 1920 women were working in the manufacture of iron and steel products and by 1930 in the production of automobiles.[120]

Wisconsin State Historical Society

Women on the assembly line at Nash Motors, Kenosha, 1917

A Wisconsin state legislative committee studied prostitution and "commercialized vice" in 1913. It used questionnaires, private detectives, and public hearings to gather data. In Superior, where there was still a segregated red light district, it found:

There were 21 houses with 8 to 10 women in each.

The rate was either $1 or $2. Half the receipts went to the madam. Prostitutes earned between $15 and $40 weekly. Many of these women supported children or other relatives. All women in the district had to be indoors between 8 p.m. and 8 a.m. Police patrolled 24 hours a day.

Other working women in Superior made the following testimony:

A telephone operator made 9¢ an hour, $30 a month.

A clerk at Woolworth's made about $9 weekly, worked 8 a.m. to 6 p.m., and until 10 p.m. on Saturdays.

A seamstress in a glove factory was paid 3½¢ per dozen pairs made, earning $6 to $7 weekly.

Only one woman interviewed, of about a dozen, had any personal savings and that only amounted to $30.[121]

"The assumption that women, however hard they work in the household and however much of actual money value that work has, do not support themselves but are supported by their husbands, that they earn nothing and own nothing — that assumption, upon which all our property laws are based, is so abominable that I cannot find words to express my opinion of it."

—Theodora W. Youmans,1915. President, Wisconsin Woman Suffrage Association.[122]

"Fifty per cent of the voters in Wisconsin are women. Men who imagine women do not want equality with men under the laws are mistaken. Men who think women voters will not use their ballots to win equality under the law are mistaken. . .Women's long fight for equal suffrage was only a means to this end — that they might use their ballots to enforce equality with men."

—Mabel Raef Putnam, 1921. President, Wisconsin chapter, National Woman's Party and Coordinator of the drive to pass a state Equal Rights Law.

American women were able to exercise their right to vote with the passage of the 19th amendment to the U.S. Constitution on August 20,1920. To many women, winning the suffrage was the ultimate victory for women's rights. Other women viewed it as but a partial victory, however; a battle won along the way to full legal equality. These women joined the National Woman's Party to fight for a federal Equal Rights Amendment. In Wisconsin, members of the Woman's Party set immediately to work to pass a *state* equal rights law — and within one year of achieving suffrage, Wisconsin women had yet another victory.[123]

Wisconsin Enacts First Equal Rights Law

MADISON,Wis., July 11,1921 — When Governor Blaine today signed the Women's Rights bill, Wisconsin became the first State in the Union where women have equal rights with men under the civil laws.

The Governor signed the historic bill, in the presence of women from several parts of the state, with a black quill pen supplied by the National Woman's Party. This pen, and a copy of the new law, are to be sent to the headquarters of the National Woman's Party in Washington, D.C. as mementoes of the first victory won by American women in their nation-wide campaign for equal civil rights.

Here is the text of the law:

"To create new section 6.015 of the statutes to remove discriminations against women and to give them equal rights before the law.

"The people of the State of Wisconsin, represented in the Senate and Assembly, do enact as follows:

"6.015. Women shall have the same rights and privileges under the law as men in the exercise of suffrage, freedom of contract, choice of residence for voting purposes, jury service, holding office, holding and conveying property, care and custody of children and in all other respects. The various courts, executive and administrative officers shall construe the statutes where the · masculine gender is used to include the feminine gender unless such construction will deny to females the special protection and privileges which they now enjoy for the general welfare. The courts, executive and administrative officers shall make all necessary rules and provisions to carry out the intent and purposes of this statute."[124]

The Wisconsin Equal Rights Law was discussed and debated by every participant in the national Equal Rights movement. While few thought that it solved all of Wisconsin women's legal problems, many feminists agreed with Wisconsin author Zona Gale that "The general grant of power lays down principles similar to those laid down in the Constitutional Bill of Rights. We know that it must be followed by specific legislation in those instances where the issues are not clear. But we hold that (the Equal Rights Law) is the necessary foundation on which to build."[125]

Critics of the Wisconsin Equal Rights Law argued that the law was too general and the provisions too vague. Worse, it left interpretation entirely up to the courts. These feminists were particularly concerned that the phrase "*unless such construction will deny females the special protection and privileges which they now enjoy for the general welfare*" would become the legal 'escape clause' through which all discriminations against women could pass. The critics proved right. By 1940 legal interpretation of the Wisconsin Equal Rights Law had rendered it meaningless as a tool for establishing equality between men and women.[126]

Zona Gale had promised that the women of Wisconsin would be "vigilant" in bringing individual statutes into accord with the Equal Rights Law. They were not. The moment passed. The Wisconsin Equal Rights Law was an empty victory.[127]

Margaret Porter Radcliffe

Every town has its 'grand ladies,' its female aristocrats who reign over the town's civic and social life. Margaret Porter Radcliffe was one such grand lady, reigning over West Allis, Wisconsin between 1904 and 1945. When Radcliffe moved to West Allis from Milwaukee she was 41 years old. Her husband was a successful businessman and her three children were in school. It was time for her to pursue her own interests and ambitions, and within one year she had laid the ground-work for a productive career as a civic leader.[128]

In the course of that career, Radcliffe served as secretary and presi-dent of the West Allis Women's Club, President of the Women's Clubs of Milwaukee County, chair of the Urban-Rural Cooperation Comm-ittee of the State Federation of Women's Clubs, Worthy Matron of the Order of the Eastern Star, vice-president of the Anti-Tuberculosis Club, chair of the 1923 Milk-for-Health Campaign, and president of the Women's Auxiliary to Milwaukee Goodwill Industries. She was al-so a member of the West Allis Library Board, the West Allis Neighbor-hood Association, the West Allis Board of Education, the Board of the First National Bank of West Allis, a founder of the Wisconsin Parent-Teachers Association, and Wisconsin's representative to the Interna-tional Congress of Women in Oslo, Norway in 1920.

If nothing else, a list like this represents an incredible number of meetings. Radcliffe might attend two or three meetings in a single day. That was her work, that was what she did. And she was not alone in this work. Many women of Radcliffe's day shared her energy and endurance and believed, as Radcliffe did, that the 'proper' place for such feminine energy was in charitable works. Rad-cliffe's life is a reminder that, contrary to popular myth, women's work in clubs has not been a casual diversion; it has often been a lifetime commit-ment. Radcliffe herself once said, "Women's clubs are not mere social clubs for the idle or curious; they are great educational centers seeking to promote the cause of edu-cation for everyone. . .They are a protest for better things."

Radcliffe not only believed in her work, she was good at it. She understood business and money, talents which she emp-loyed as a fundraiser for count-less causes and as bookkeeper for the Radcliffe Manufacturing Company. As a member of the building committee of the West Allis Library Board, Radcliffe was the main advocate of the 'Carnegie plan' of financing and was the one who approached the Carnegie Foundation for library funds and arranged the receipt of those funds in 1912. Four years later, she raised funds locally to build a second branch of the West Allis library.

Radcliffe was equally talented as an organizer — of individuals, groups, causes, and campaigns. It seems she must have organized everyone in West Allis at some time. She organized the city's poor women into a Home Industries Association through which they made goods in their homes and sold them. She organized the city's mothers into a Parent-Teacher Association to study proper methods of child-rearing. She even organized 40 teenage boys into a 'gardening squad' which turned a West Allis vacant lot into a flower and vegetable garden in the summer of 1915.

One of Radcliffe's greatest organizational feats was the *Milwaukee Sentinel's* Cooking School which was begun in cooperation with the Milwaukee County General Federation of Women's Clubs the year Radcliffe was its president. Because of her great success in setting up the school, she continued as its organizer for five years, from 1925 to 1930. The 'school' was a two-day convention, attracting over 30,000 women from all over Wisconsin. The participants attended lectures in food preparation, nutrition, entertaining, etc. According to Radcliffe, the school was a "vital factor in the happiness and harmony of Wisconsin homes."

The irony in this is that Radcliffe herself hated to cook and seldom did it. And while she was widely known for her speeches on professional motherhood and the beauty of mother love, she was not particularly maternal in her own family. Though she devoted herself to the cause of improving the home and uplifting the mother for the sake of the child, she herself was an (unpaid) career woman, out of her home much of the time, employing servants to take care of the housework and depending upon her three children to take care of themselves.

These apparent contradictions in Radcliffe's life can be found in the lives of many conservative Progressive women who believed that women's traditional roles could be 'professionalized' and believed that modern life would be better for it. Radcliffe saw her own role in this conservative reform movement as that of a leader, a woman apart. An aristocrat by nature *and* ambitious by nature, Radcliffe had to coordinate these two instincts in work that would be both active and conservative. Her 40-year career as an advocate for the home, mother, and child served well to satisfy her own energetic drives without challenging the traditional social structure. And just as the contradictions in Radcliffe's life were an important part of her times; so her contribution to the state and demonstration of women's ability to organize and direct are an important part of Wisconsin women's history.

Part IV: The Twenties and Beyond

The thread of American women's history stretching between 1920 and 1960 is much too complex to summarize in a few paragraphs. Nevertheless, this 40-year period does constitute a kind of unit in that it was the first time since the 1840's that American women had no structured 'women's movement' to turn to. In the illusion of victory that accompanied the winning of woman suffrage, women all over the country came to believe that they now had full equality, that their work was done. Women continued to be active, of course, but their energies were not directed toward the cause of womankind in particular. More commonly, women were told — and agreed — to use their new citizenship for the good of others: the poor, the sick, the needy and the young. Particularly the young. Women in Wisconsin, like women all over the U.S., were encouraged to devote themselves to the nation's children, either as mothers, teachers, civic leaders, or volunteer workers.

Not all women abandoned the women's rights movement after 1920; but the few who continued with the movement as a *political* force were essentially confined to the National Woman's Party and its unending fight for a federal Equal Rights Amendment. And those women who carried the spirit of the free and liberated 'New Woman' into the 1930's were usually considered 'bohemian;' they were the artists, writers, poets and painters.

Though lacking any conscious women's movement during this period, American women did continue to benefit from the gains made by earlier women activists. They now had more education, more social freedom and somewhat better job opportunities. These improvements equipped women to cope more effectively with the exigencies of their own lives, but without a consciousness of women's rights, the women of this period were not prepared to work toward improving their 'lot' or toward restructuring traditional sex roles.

The effect of the Depression and World War II was to make it unpatriotic for women to take jobs from men. But these two events also made it economically necessary for many women to work. Caught in this double bind, women found that working for pay was acceptable if you *needed* it or if you wished to *serve society*. It was a rare woman in this era who had the courage to say she wanted a paying job for the sake of her independence, talent or ambition.

Between 1930 and 1960 an average of 30% of American women worked at paid jobs outside the home. The other 70% worked — and worked hard — at unpaid jobs inside the home and within the community. (Volunteer community work did have its rewards; it may have gone unpaid but it was one "acceptable" form of work outside the home). It took the women's movement of the 1960's and '70's to demand recognition for all that these female volunteer workers accomplished, but that recognition is beginning to come. Coming too, is the realization that the myth and the reality of modern women's history are two very different things. While the myth of this period was that woman's-place-is-in-the-home, the reality was that most women were outside the home — either through choice or necessity. The activities of .these paid and unpaid working women were not organized or consciously feminist or very well publicized. They were individual responses to life. But through their work, this era's women made inestimable contributions to their communities, to their families, and to women's history. Not only did they leave an interesting record of achievement; they raised a generation of daughters who expected to be equal, active participants in the work of life.

Ida Pope Ehle

Long after public schools had become firmly established in Wisconsin's cities and towns, rural school systems were struggling to find teachers and draw students off the farm and into the classroom. Ida Pope Ehle was one of those who fought the battle for universal education in northern Wisconsin.[129]

As a teacher in the rural schools of Price County for 21 years, Ehle came to know the farmers in the area, came to know how to talk to them, how to convince them to let their sons and daughters leave the farm work for a while and go to high school in town. Letting a teenager go off to high school put an economic burden on farmers; if they were going to agree to it at all, Ehle had to find jobs for the children in town and a place to stay. She performed this free counseling/employment/social work service for countless families in Price County. "It got so that her friends would run when they saw her coming because they knew she wanted them to take in another student," recalls her daughter, Marguerite Ehle Ellsworth of Milwaukee. And when she could find no one to take students, she took them in herself. The Ehle home housed at least a half a dozen students over the years, along with the four Ehle children, three of the children's cousins, and one adopted daughter (who spoke only Bohemian when she arrived but learned English in three weeks).

Ida Ehle's husband, Edward, was a logger, an outdoorsman, and a lover of children. "He never went anyplace in Phillips without a couple of kids on each arm." The Ehle's life together was a hard one, but happy. "I had no idea we were poor," says Ellsworth, "we had books and music." Evenings at home, Ida Ehle would play the piano and sing, or read Dickens or Shakespeare to Edward Ehle and the children. It sounds like an idyllic life, but it was a constant struggle just to keep food on the table for all those children and all the friends the Ehles liked to have around the house. The family needed two incomes and Ida Ehle returned to teaching in the Price County schools soon after the birth of her fourth child.

"I remember Mama when I was a small girl," says Ellsworth, "building the fire when we got to the little log school that was her first teaching job after returning to that work. After school we helped wash the blackboards and sweep." Sometimes Ehle's teaching jobs were beyond commuting distance from Phillips; in those cases she took the children off to school with her and they all came back to Phillips on the weekends.

This was not a new pace for Ehle. Her father had died when she was 10 and her mother was dead before she turned 16. After graduation with the first class of Medford High in 1889, 17-year-old Ida Pope was employed in a Price County school where she taught eight grades and earned $18 per month. She supplemented her income by clerking in a store on Saturdays and in this way was able to support her two younger sisters and younger brother through high school. Ida Pope was 25 when she married Edward Ehle. Two years later, in 1899, the Ehles moved to Phillips and within six years of marriage they had four children.

Ida Ehle's lifelong devotion to the education of the children of Price County is commendable in itself; what is even more extraordinary was her devotion to her own education. According to her daughter, "She went to school whenever she had the opportunity." Usually this meant summer school at Price County Normal, which she attended long and diligently until she finally obtained a diploma in 1917. The diploma from normal school allowed Ehle to teach in town, at Phillips High School, which she did for two years. But her own education was still not complete. To earn a bachelor's degree she went to summer school at Stevens Point State University and, in 1922, she left home for a year of residency at Stevens Point. Ehle obtained her college degree at the end of that year when she was 50 years old. The commitment to see her through college had been shared by the entire family and must have put a tremendous strain on the Ehle's meagre resources. "When I think of how shabby she was in appearance," recalls her daughter, adding, "Mother would buy books when she should have bought shoes."

Armed with her degree, Ehle was qualified to take on more responsibility in the schools of Price County. She served for two years as County Superintendent of Schools, driving around in a little old Ford to inspect schools and supervise curriculum. After that, she was named Principal of the Forest County Teachers' Training School at Crandon where she worked for another two years. But Ehle's health was failing and she had to retire long before she was ready to. All the years of work to get where she wanted to be had taken their toll. Ida Ehle died of heart failure at the age of 57. Trying to explain the early death of this remarkably strong woman, her daughter said "it was like she was worn out."

***

Shortly after woman suffrage was granted, Grace Pilgrim Bloom ran for county board in Polk County. She was elected and became the first and only woman to serve on the Polk County Board to this day. In an interview in 1973, Bloom recalled why she did not run for a second term:

"I did not like the work because of sex discrimination. I was put on such a minor committee. I objected to hearing my femininity used as an issue. I had the same interest in county affairs as the men, but was given no opportunity to assert myself."[130]

Sr. Mary Victoria

Sr. Mary Victoria arrived at Bayfield, Wisconsin in October, 1890 to teach in the Indian schools in town and on the Red Cliff Indian Reservation. At 22, she was still two years away from taking her final vows in the order of the Sisters of St. Francis. But her superiors at the mother house in Joliet, Illinois sent the young novitiate to Wisconsin for some "practical teaching experience." She stayed for 67 years, teaching well over 2,000 children and often four or five generations of the same family.[131]

Sr. Victoria was made a member of the Chippewa tribe and honored on the occasion of both her 50th and 60th anniversaries at Red Cliff. Her career is interesting, not only for the dedication it reflects, but for the great span of history that it covers. By the time she retired in 1957, Sr. Victoria had experienced every kind of hardship and reward that typically befell Wisconsin's rural parochial schools.

Born Ida Steidl in Chicago in 1868, Sr. Victoria had wanted to be a sister for as long as she could remember. At age 17 she went to the Sisters of St. Francis in Joliet, becoming an apostulant at 18 and a novice at 19. When Sr. Victoria first went to Bayfield, she and her colleague Sr. Seraphica were responsible for teaching at the Industrial School for Indian Girls in Bayfield and for teaching the elementary school at the Red Cliff Reservation three miles away. This meant a round-trip journey every day for six years. "These trips were a pasttime when the weather was fair," recalled Sr. Victoria in later years, "but nothing of the kind during the long cold winters." Sometimes the sisters made the trip on foot, sometimes by horse, sometimes in a cutter, one of the most dangerous modes of conveyance ever invented. In winter, the cutter often tipped over, dumping the Missionary sisters unceremoniously in the snow. During the rainy season, "losing rubbers in the sticky clay and being spattered from head to foot was no novelty."

In 1893, the U.S. government sold the Red Cliff Indian School to a railroad company and refused to build another school where Catholic nuns would be teaching. The church put up a log cabin school and the sisters were able to continue teaching at Red Cliff, occasionally using the caboose on the new Bayfield Transfer Railroad for transportation. By 1896, the Church had convinced the government to sponsor the Red Cliff School as it was the only school on the reservation, and to pay the sisters' salaries. Sr. Victoria and Sr. Seraphica moved to Red Cliff in 1896 and taught in the government-sponsored school until 1922.

In 1922 the government withdrew its sponsorship and the Red Cliff school became, again, a thoroughly parochial school — but with no financial support. Sr. Seraphica retired in 1922, ending her close 33-year relationship with Sr. Victoria. Sr. Victoria became the principal of the Red Cliff School as well as one of the teachers, but her main job was fund-raising. She solicited clothes from friends in Chicago and St. Paul and conducted a rummage sale every month which usually netted about $75. The school received additional support from benefactors, including Sr. Victoria's own brothers who had inherited their father's meat-packing plant in Matoon, Illinois. Sr. Victoria lived without a salary during these years but was supported by the people of Red Cliff who, according to her, "willingly gave the last cent in their pockets to help the church and the school." The Depression made life even harder in Red Cliff. "We are poor, very poor," wrote Sr. Victoria in 1931. "The logging camps are closed because there is no sale for lumber, the fishing is a failure because there is no sale for fish."

Things began to improve in the late '30's and '40's. Then disaster struck again in 1947 when the Old Red Cliff school and convent burned to the ground. While new accomodations were being constructed, school was held in the Reservation's community hall and the sisters lived in what was left of the old church basement — the "Dugout" — where "blankets were strung up to separate the different rooms. They were exactly like war refugees in bombed out Europe but they did it gladly. . .to serve their children here."

Sr. Victoria celebrated her 60th anniversary at Red Cliff in the new school and stayed to teach for seven more years before retiring to the mother house in Joliet where she died in 1962. The outpouring of love and admiration that is evident in the speeches made on Sr. Victoria's 50th and 60th anniversaries, her retirement, and her death, bespeak a great deal more than simple respect for a daughter of the Church. There was a genuine feeling among the Chippewa of Red Cliff that Sr. Victoria had sacrificed and endured far beyond the call of duty for their sakes. She was made an honorary member of the Chippewa tribe in the 1940's in recognition of her "constant struggle to educate our minds and free our souls."

Marie Francek Illichmann

The women working at the Hurley Washing Machine Factory in 1923 were there for dozens of reasons; some to support themselves, some to support others, some to get away from home, others to get a home. Marie Francek Illichmann was there so her two children could attend high school in the city. There was no high school near the Illichmann farm in Ormsby, Wisconsin so every fall, from 1921 to 1924, Marie Illichmann packed up the children and moved south to Chicago where she could find a job and they could get the education she had never had.[132]

Marie Francek Illichmann was born in Czechoslovakia in 1877. The third of 12 children in a working class family, she went to work as a serving girl at age 14. She wanted to become a teacher, but her father refused to take the 'charity' that would have enabled Marie to finish school. She always regretted her lack of education and, like many immigrants, was ashamed of it. For example, even though Illichmann learned to read, write and speak English as an adult, she never uttered a word of English around her children. She spoke only Czech, explains her daughter, "because she was afraid of making an error (in English) in front of us."

Marie Francek had come to the U.S. when she was 26 to care for a sickly brother in Chicago. Within three years she had met and married Stephen Illichmann, a Czech locksmith and iron worker. The couple did well; Stephen Illichmann was promoted to superintendent of his plant, Marie Illichmann bore two healthy children, and they were able to buy a two-story house.

In 1917 Stephen Illichmann got "the farm bug" and bought a farm near Ormsby, in northern Wisconsin's Langlade County. Neither of the Illichmanns knew anything about farming; Marie Illichmann had never lived on a farm. Animals frightened her. Moreover, she feared that moving to rural Wisconsin would make it impossible for her children to attend high school. According to the Illichmann's daughter, Blanche Mendl, "all her pleading and tears were of no avail." The Illichmanns moved to Ormsby — but not before Marie had exacted a pledge from Stephen that the children *would* complete their education.

The move to Ormsby was a bit premature. As soon as the family was settled on the farm, Stephen Illichmann had to return to Chicago to earn needed money — leaving Marie and the children (aged 9 and 10) with an uncle "who knew about as much about farming as we did."

"There were six cows but no milk all winter," writes Mendl, "a dozen ancient hens but no eggs. None of us knew how to start and keep a fire going in the old box stove. We pumped water outside, had a privy with a Sears Roebuck catalogue in the middle of the garden, and flickering kerosene lights. Quite a change from the city. . .Mother hated it but took it in stride. . .Fortunately she had insisted on bringing barrels of flour and sugar from Chicago. . .It was her ingenuity in making delicious meals out of things we had on hand that kept us alive."

The next few years were busy ones. Stephen earned money in lumber camps, coming home on weekends. Marie and the children tended the farm. In a short time they had become quite skillful with livestock. Marie Illichmann successfully raised chickens, geese, ducks, pigs and bees. "Mother cared for them all, worked in the fields and cared for the garden from which she canned food for winter."

The Illichmanns also kept busy in the Czech community that had grown up in Langlade County. Members of the Z.C.B.J. — the Western Bohemian Fraternal Association — the Illichmanns participated in banquets and plays and songfests to raise money and promote fellowship. Marie Illichmann's devotion to her children's education included a determination that they learn their cultural heritage. Holidays were always celebrated in the traditional Czech way and the children were encouraged to participate in Czech activities around the state.

By 1921 it was time for the children to attend high school but the Langlade County High School was in Antigo, 14 miles away. The Illichmanns could not afford to board the children in Antigo, nor did they have a vehicle that could traverse the county roads through mud and ice. Holding her husband to his promise, however, Marie Illichmann arranged for the children to attend school in Chicago. The two teenagers went south alone and stayed with relatives for the first few weeks. Their mother joined them when she was done with the harvesting at Ormsby. In the spring she returned to Ormsby before the children so she could help with the planting. This pattern was repeated for three years during which time Marie Illichmann was the sole support of herself and her children while in Chicago.

Different arrangements had to be made each year, new jobs found, new flats rented. The first year Illichmann worked as a cook in a restaurant for a little cash, meals and a room. The next year she did piece work in a tailor shop. The third and final year in Chicago was the year Illichmann found work at the Hurley Washing Machine Factory. It was piece work, and Illichmann's hands were made raw from the grease and kerosene, but it paid better than the tailor shop and was just two blocks from their flat.

Through all of this — through all the work and worry, through all the travel and planning, through all the tonsilitis and pneumonia and measles — through it all, Marie Illichmann kept hold of the things she valued most. She bought a piano for her daughter and paid for lessons out of what little money she had. On weekends she took the children to museums and parks; and in the evenings she read aloud — at the same time "her hands were flying, knitting socks and many times sweaters with designs, without missing a stitch." She made most of the family's clothes, knitted sweaters and crocheted everything from underclothes to bedspreads. She even tanned rabbit skins to make blankets, coats, hats, leggings, gloves and house slippers.

Marie Illichmann's efforts to insure her children's education ultimately resulted in son Steve attending Ripon College and the University of Chicago and daughter Blanche attending Langlade Normal School. Both children became teachers. Marie Illichmann had accomplished her goal. Her children were equipped with a complete American education and a full Czech heritage. In her 83 years she stretched herself to bridge time and place, to make her children's life richer and to make their growth possible. Without women like Illichmann to act as such bridges, the gaps in our society's culture and education would have been insurmountable.

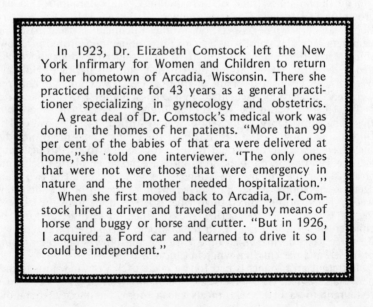

In 1923, Dr. Elizabeth Comstock left the New York Infirmary for Women and Children to return to her hometown of Arcadia, Wisconsin. There she practiced medicine for 43 years as a general practitioner specializing in gynecology and obstetrics.

A great deal of Dr. Comstock's medical work was done in the homes of her patients. "More than 99 per cent of the babies of that era were delivered at home," she told one interviewer. "The only ones that were not were those that were emergency in nature and the mother needed hospitalization."

When she first moved back to Arcadia, Dr. Comstock hired a driver and traveled around by means of horse and buggy or horse and cutter. "But in 1926, I acquired a Ford car and learned to drive it so I could be independent."

Dr. Rosa Minoka Hill

She was born a Mohawk and died an Oneida. She was raised in the city and lived on a farm. She was trained as a Quaker but chose to be a Catholic. She left her medical practice in Philadelphia to become a Wisconsin farm wife. And she practiced medicine all her life. Dr. Rosa Minoka Hill was her own person. The story of her life is a story of choices made, paths selected; for all the twists of fate she endured, she was never a victim of circumstance.

In 1880, four-year-old Lillie Minoka was taken from her parents' medicine show tent in Philadelphia. Her parents were dying and Dr. J. Allen, a Quaker physician who had worked among the Mohawks, took Lillie and placed her in the Grahame Institute, a Quaker school for girls in Philadelphia. There she was raised by Dr. Allen and by 'Aunt Nan' Grahame (who called her Rosa because they thought she looked more like a rose than a lily).[134]

In 1896, Rosa entered Woman's Medical College in Philadelphia. She was only the second American Indian to study there. Licensed in 1900, after an internship at Woman's Hospital, Hill opened an office in Philadelphia with another woman and built up a busy practice during her first five years as a physician. But during those five years she also grew to love a young Oneida from Wisconsin named Charles Hill.

In 1905, Hill hesitatingly asked Rosa to leave her practice and go with him to Wisconsin as his wife. Hill did not want his wife to practice medicine professionally in Oneida; he knew he was asking Rosa to give up a great deal, but he believed a wife's proper work was in the home. Rosa accepted Charles Hill's offer, deferring to his beliefs on a wife's role.

The transition from Philadelphia to Oneida was slow and difficult for Rosa Minoka Hill. She had to learn everything, from how to light a wood stove and pump water to planting and caring for a vegetable garden. She also had to learn the ways of Indian people. Though an Indian herself, she was a foreigner among the rural Oneidas, not only because of her city ways but because they knew she practiced "white man's medicine." Medical care for the Oneidas was seriously deficient, there was only one doctor for approximately 1,500 Indians in the area and an old government hospital which the Oneidas called "The House of Death." Rosa Hill was busy enough learning to be a farm wife, but she took time to learn about traditional Indian cures, the use of herbs and berries as medicine and the Oneidas' feelings about disease and death. In this way, Hill built up trust in the community and within a year she was being called upon to tend sick babies, care for wounds and treat illness, often using a combination of Indian medicines and whatever white man's medicines she could obtain. She worked to develop the Oneidas' trust of white man's medicine because she felt it was unethical for her to not use what she had learned in medical school. In time she had earned the respect of the area's doctor and tribal medicine man.

Between 1906 and 1915, Rosa Hill bore six children; the last two were twin girls born in the fall of 1915. Life on the Hill farm was a struggle, but the family was happy and hardworking; Charles with his farming and Rosa with her children and her neighborly doctoring. When the twins were five months old, Charles died from a sudden attack of appendicitis. Rosa was left with the six children, the house, the farm, three horses, two cows, and some chickens. Fortunately, she had a small trust fund from Dr. Allen's estate and that income, plus goods which patients occasionally brought in 'payment' for Hill's medical services, kept the family alive.

World War I took the Oneidas' one official doctor, leaving Rosa Hill as the only trained physician in the community. She was now practicing medicine full-time in her 'kitchen clinic.' She had no license to practice in Wisconsin so could not charge patients a fee or obtain drugs by herself. Nevertheless she managed, with the cooperation of doctors in Green Bay, to attend to the medical needs of both whites and Indians in the Oneida area. Over the years this unflappable woman took charge of the influenza epidemic of 1918, saw to countless births, injuries, and illnesses, traveled thousands of miles by buggy over icy roads to reach patients or get medicine, and faced endless cases of tuberculosis and malnutrition, two of the ever-present realities of Indian life.

Hill's trust fund collapsed with the stock market crash of 1929 and financial conditions in Oneida became more serious. Without a license she could not be paid for treating people on welfare. Hill did have the garden for food; but she always needed money to buy medicines. Not having that medical license was becoming more and more of a burden. The Hill children convinced their mother to take the exam for a Wisconsin Medical License — 35 years after her graduation from medical college. Hill had to borrow the money to pay the exam fee and had only four months to study before going to Madison for the two-day ordeal in the fall of 1934. She was one of the five, out of nine candidates, licensed that year. She returned to Oneida as Dr. Rosa Minoka Hill, M.D. She was now 58 years old.

Nothing changed very much after Hill was licensed. A box full of unpaid bills indicates that she did not use her license to collect many fees. She continued to simply accept whatever was offered in payment, always sensitive to the fact that even the poorest Indian had pride. Medical service improved in the 1930's simply because Dr. Hill could now obtain needed drugs more easily and by 1939 she had the assistance of a public health nurse three days a week and a government doctor once a week. The government also began to provide the Oneidas with certain food supplies which helped ease the community-wide malnutrition that Hill was constantly battling.

A heart attack in 1946 forced the 69-year-old Hill to slow down; she stopped making house calls. But her kitchen clinic was busy with patients from morning 'til night right up to the time of Hill's death in 1952. The last years of her life had brought Dr. Hill many awards and honors from both medical and Indian groups. In 1947 she received the Indian Achievement Award for her philanthropy from the Indian Council Fire, and in 1948 the Oneida community erected a monument in her honor. The American Medical Society recognized her in 1949 on the 50th anniversary of her graduation from Women's Medical College, she was the first woman to be made an honorary member of the Wisconsin Medical Association, and was honored by the U.W. College of Agriculture for her service to rural people. But Hill's greatest honor probably came to her in 1947 when she was made a member of the Oneida tribe. Chief Julius Danforth said at the ceremony, "She has labored long among us. We feel humble that all we can do in return is to adopt her into the tribe. It is little at this late date."

Minnie Pearl Potter

"One winter night, early in the years of the great Depression, a horse and cutter pulled up in front of a large frame house at the edge of the village of Radisson, Wisconsin. The wind was strong, drifting snow, and the air was freezing cold. The beginning of a real Wisconsin blizzard. A night to stay home and pull your chair up close to the fire. This particular house was that of the midwife, Mrs. Otis Potter, and when someone came for her she went, no matter what.

"The driver of the cutter went up to the spacious porch of the Roselawn Maternity Home and knocked on the door. Minnie Potter answered immediately. She was an attractive woman, calm and self-assured. She took only a few minutes getting ready, collecting her bag and a heavy quilt to bundle up in, and then she went out into the storm. They drove into the countryside making progress slowly, but finally came to a tiny farmhouse far away from its neighbors. Mrs. Potter made her way through the deep snow and into the house. She greeted the expectant mother cheerfully, removed her wraps, added wood to the fire and put the kettle on. Sometime later, twins were born.

"This same night, a mother of ten was expecting her eleventh child. She was alone, abandoned by her husband. She sent word for Mrs. Potter to come, and as always when needed, Mrs. Potter came. The eleventh child was born, with difficulty, its mother's life in great danger. Through a long exhausting night and well into the morning, Mrs. Potter fought diligently, using skill wrought through years of experience to save the life of the mother. All ended well and before she left for home that morning, Mrs. Potter brought order to the household and prepared a hot, nourishing breakfast for the large brood. Leaving the eldest boy in charge, she left, breaking trail through deep snow to the road and the buggy awaiting her. Exhausted, Mrs. Potter arrived home, walked into her living room, and suffered the first of several strokes."[136]

Minnie Pearl Rathbun Potter was the nurse and midwife to the people of northern Wisconsin's Sawyer County for almost 40 years, from 1918 until 1954. In that time she delivered over 2,000 babies and never lost a mother. Though she had no formal medical training, Potter read medical textbooks and journals throughout her life. These, plus common sense, experience, and a 'special touch' made Potter invaluable to the people of Sawyer County. There was a doctor in Winter (12 miles away) and one in Ladysmith (25 miles away), but both of these men depended on Potter to diagnose cases and determine if a doctor was needed. "She could usually tell ahead of time if there were going to be complications (in a birth) and would call a doctor or take the mother to the hospital . . . Doctors used to say they hated to take a case Mrs. Potter had given up on." She worked closely with the doctors in the area, "Doc Smith would circumcise boy babies at the Roselawn Maternity Home using Mrs. Potter's dining room table."[137]

It cost $5 to have 'Grandma Potter' deliver your baby, and $1 a day to stay at her maternity home. "I had several babies there. Stayed a week or two each time. I enjoyed it very much. She cooked for you.

She was a good cook . . . and a jolly woman. I remember we'd sit in the living room working on quilts, waiting . . . Times were very hard and most people couldn't pay. She took them anyway."[138]

When Potter was paid, it was usually with vegetables or chickens or some sort of service. The Potters never had much cash but they owned 40 acres right in town, much of it planted in corn and potatoes and a large garden. Mrs. Potter had beautiful flower beds, roses, and a large lawn — hence the name, Roselawn Maternity Home. She did all the gardening herself, as well as tending to the chickens, geese, and cows. "A patient would come and if there was nothing else to eat, Mrs. Potter would get a chicken, wring its neck and fix it for dinner."[139]

The Potters had four children — three sons and a daughter — and had been married in 1896 when Minnie Pearl Rathbun was only 15. The couple farmed in several Wisconsin counties before moving to Radisson in 1918. "Mr. Potter did not live in the house but in one of the buildings nearby which he called his 'Bunkhouse.' He worked in the woods, off and on, and I remember him making sleds and toys for kids."[140]

It was said that Minnie Potter had a 'way' with babies. "She had a touch about her; she kept sick babies at her home and had cribs there just like in a hospital. She had untold patience with them."[141] She also had a way of combining sound medical practices with homemade ingenuity. "Premature or very small babies she wrapped in blankets and laid in a box on the oven door to be kept warm . . . When babies had diarrhea, she'd boil blackberry roots and fix 'em up good."[142]

Babies were not Potter's only patients, however. "Her nursing ability saved countless lives during the flu epidemic of 1917-18. Southern Sawyer County was without doctors in World War I and the people relied on Minnie Potter. It seemed that God gave her the strength and stamina she needed during this trying time. Many in the area can thank Mrs. Potter for keeping them alive." "She acted as a hometown doctor going from house to house during the epidemic when in some households every member of the family was sick and there was no one to take care of them or even to clean up after them. She nursed them, saw that there was food to eat and put their house in order."[143]

During all her years caring for the sick, Potter never had her own means of transportation. "People who needed her would come after her or send someone else . . . Grimh's Power Co. had about the first car in Radisson and Mrs. Potter would call Alma Grimh to take her to a patient and off they would go as far as they could by car and walk the rest of the way."[144]

Because of a series of strokes, Grandma Potter spent the last years of her life confined to a wheelchair, living for a while with her son and then with her daughter. She died in a Waupaca hospital in December, 1954 and was buried in Radisson. The funeral for her had to be held in a churchyard as the crowd could not fit into any of the town's churches.[145] In eulogizing her, one former recipient of her care said: "Many will be remembered in the economic, educational, social and religious development of this area, but only one will be remembered for guiding the birth, health, and death of the people here, that one is Minnie Potter."[146]

Eulalia Croll

When Eulalia Croll was a senior at U.W.-Madison in 1913, she was the captain of six athletic teams: baseball, basketball, field hockey, tennis, bowling, and volleyball. She lettered in all six sports that year, but her enduring love was basketball which she continued to play until she was 50 years old. "I always played guard," she recalls today. "I wasn't tall, but I was wide!"[147]

Despite her enthusiasm for athletics, Croll was not able to major in physical education at U.W. "I didn't even consider it," she explains, because there was no physical education major for women at the University at the time. But Croll was as talented at mathematics and music as she was at sports. She divided her time between majoring in math, participating in sports and playing the piano for the women's exercise and modern dance classes. She also helped the struggling young women's physical education program by keeping the department's books.

Croll does not recall that women athletes were particularly teased about their activities in college; the department at U.W. was new and people were excited about the potential for sports to improve women's health. Blanche Trilling, the head of the Women's Physical Education Department from its beginning in 1912 until 1946, believed that women's athletics should be recreational, not competitive. The women's athletic program was designed to provide "sports for everyone" through an intramural program which involved class teams in every sport.[148] Croll remembers trying to play baseball with the senior class team on the flattened tier in the middle of Bascom Hill, and hearing crowds of cheering fans at the women's basketball games in Lathrop Hall.

Upon graduation from the University, 24-year-old Croll returned to her home in Manitowoc to work as a math teacher at a local high school. There was little time for sports. "I had my music then," says Croll, who played organ at the Lutheran and, later, the Presbyterian church and participated in a Monday night music club. Croll soon decided that she did not like teaching and became, instead, a bookkeeper. When her father died in 1927, Croll and her mother moved to Milwaukee and in 1928 she went to work at the Boston Store. Her experience at her father's fruit and vegetable store in Manitowoc prepared Croll to take a new position as head of the Boston Store's telephone department, a position which she was to hold for 35 years.

Croll was 36 when she moved to Milwaukee and decided to resume her athletic 'career'. Within weeks of her arrival she had volunteered to score for the city recreation department, making her one of three women scorekeepers in the city. In ten years as a scorekeeper, she worked over 1,000 games — mostly girls' softball, but some girls' basketball and some boys' softball as well.

She was as active on the court as on the sidelines during those years, having organized both a basketball and a baseball team among the women employees at the Boston Store. For nearly 10 years the teams competed in the Milwaukee Women's Industrial League, capturing the League championship in basketball in 1940 and 1942 and the baseball championship in 1938 and 1940. Croll served as player-coach for both teams, keeping her position as guard in basketball and playing catcher in baseball. "The other women weren't as interested as I was," Croll says now. "I had to do a lot of pushing to get them to stay on the team and attend practices." She managed to maintain the enthusiasm for ten years, but when she stopped playing in the 1940's, the other women stopped playing too.

Croll continued to score young people's games for the city of Milwaukee until the 1960's, going out to all parts of town in all kinds of weather until she was at least 75. Retired from the Boston Store at 72, Croll found that she still had too much energy to stop working altogether. For the past ten years she has worked at an answering service in Milwaukee, keeping the books and records. She is 84 now, still walks to and from work every day, in all seasons, still loves basketball and the Chicago Cubs. "I owe my good health to my athletics," she says proudly, adding, "I've enjoyed everything in athletics, but I liked it best when I could play."

<hr />

"Mary Jean Malotte was an enthusiastic log roller from the age of five. She, with her brother Joe, . . . started giving exhibitions at the age of six, at first making only local appearances and gradually broadening the field until in August, 1938, she took first place at Escanaba, Michigan.

"Mary Jean, who was known as the 'Backwoods Girl from Wisconsin,' never took her log rolling seriously until she won the world championship, after which she paid all her expenses for school and college as a birler . . . she took her books on her trips and thus kept up with her studies. She graduated from Cornell High School in 1940 and later entered theological school in Indiana, where she became a minister in the Church of God. Even as a minister, in July, 1947, she retained her title of World Champion Log Birler at a meet in Gladstone, Michigan."

Florence Howard, Cornell librarian.
Quoted in Our Wisconsin Heritage
by Bertha K. Whyte.[149]

Margery Latimer

*"There's only one possession that's worth having
and that is the capacity to feel that life is a privilege
and that each person in it is unique and will never
appear again."*
—*Margery Latimer to Zona Gale, 1928*[150]
*"Of all the young writers whose work has come to
my attention over a period of years, none had anything like the promise of Margery Latimer."*
—*Zona Gale, August 17, 1932*[151]

Margery Latimer was born in Portage, Wisconsin in 1899, lived there
until she was 18 and returned when she was 30. In the interim she lived
in New York City's Greenwich Village, became involved in some of the
most radical social movements of her day, and wrote three books which
made her a rising star in the literary world. Latimer kept in touch with
Portage through her friend and mentor, Zona Gale, one of Wisconsin's
best-known authors and Portage's most celebrated citizen. Latimer
recalled that she began her friendship with Gale when she was in high
school. "Zona saw one of my stories in the village paper and from that
time she gave hours and hours to me, listening to my work and only
telling me what she liked, never what she didn't like. I had no friends
except her. I lived in the illusion she made for me."[152]

Latimer was a product and an expression of the romanticism of the
1920's. Deeply spiritual and philosophic, she was also impulsive and
high-spirited. She attended U.W.-Madison for two years, trying to major
in English . . . "but I got so miserable over everyone telling me that I
didn't know reality and that I could never earn my living that I went to
New York and got a job doing everything no one else wanted to do in
the fashion department of the *Woman's Home Companion.* I was fired
after eight months. I went back to the University of Wisconsin as a
Zona Gale Scholar."[153]

Gale gave scholarships each year to writers with promise and it was
as a recipient of one of those scholarships that Latimer intensified her
relationship with Gale. But she only stayed at U.W. for one year before
returning to New York, "where I took an apartment in the artists'
colony — Greenwich Village."[154] Latimer was 22 now, living the life of
the struggling young artist, trying to eat and pay the rent by typing
manuscripts and reviewing books. She managed to survive on a meagre
income, writing to Gale, "I'm getting along very well indeed. Lula paid
me five dollars and I bought a raincoat, green, an umbrella and rubbers.
I love them."[155]

Latimer was writing short stories during this period and getting them
published in magazines and collections. But she was also experiencing
all the pain and self-doubt and genuine terror that seems to haunt
artists. Her correspondence with Zona Gale through these years is
important, not because Gale was famous but because the two women
shared a relationship of depth and intensity. It was to Gale that Latimer
revealed herself and through her relationship with Gale that we can
see her struggle to grow as a woman and as an artist.

"Dearest Zona," wrote Latimer shortly after moving back to New York, *"Your story in* Harper's Bazaar! *I don't understand — is there really a class of men in the world who actually wants marriage? Is there any woman in the world who can interest a man through her superiority? A thousand times no is what I say. Businessmen, perhaps, want performance. But the sensitive kind are different. For example, I am relatively speaking a superior person, I should think — simply because of what I know about myself and my dreams. (But) if I expect to fulfill myself, if I want a child, I will have to go out into the streets and ask someone. That's the truth: I will have to face it alone, support it and myself. Why? Simply because sensitive men are afraid of responsibility and they will not stoop to owning or being owned."*[156]

Like most of the 'bohemian' New Women of her day, Latimer suffered greatly from what seemed to her to be mutually exclusive desires for love with a 'sensitive man' and a lifestyle that could include a child. She reflected her generation's view of marriage-as-bondage, at the same time revealing her artistic vision, in another letter to Gale, written almost six years later:

"I had a dream recently that has weakened me more than anything in my life . . . I was standing on a marble porch, one without a roof, all smooth white marble, and it stretched into the sea and the sea was the blue you look far into and the sky was the same blue. The sky moved over me in a sea of waves and the sea moved in cloud waves. There was the blinding white of marble and the too-intense blue of water and air. My mother was standing beside me in a blue dress, a band around her neck, and suddenly I took hold of her wrists and said in a voice that took my whole body, "I promise you I shall never marry."[157]

Much has been made of the mentor/protege relationship between Gale and Latimer, mainly because two of Latimer's books include unattractive characters who were supposedly patterned after Zona Gale. Critics interpreted this as a sign of Latimer's vicious rejection of Gale, and Latimer herself suffered tremendous guilt for casting her dearest friend in such an unkind light. But Gale understood that Latimer had to reject her as a mentor if they were ever to become truly equals in their relationship. Gale understood, too, that "your sense of struggle is not between you and me, it is between you and your self. That self and I are as much one as we ever were."[158]

Still, for all the love and understanding, it was a stormy friendship, mostly because Latimer was a stormy person. "Tall, red-haired, very much alive and vigorous," wrote one interviewer, Margery Latimer impresses one with her vitality."[159] Between 1928 and 1931, Latimer published three highly acclaimed books: *We Are Incredible* (1928), which she wrote during a six-week stay in Portage; *Nellie Bloom and Other Stories* (1929), which included "The Family," declared by some to be the "the strongest short story published in America in a quarter of a century;"[160] and *This is My Body* (1931). As an author, Latimer wanted "farm women and cleaning women and maiden aunts and people who have tremendous things happen to them like my work . . . In *We Are Incredible* I wrote of life and doom. But that's not how I really feel. I want to write of life more as it really is — as being a privilege and a joy."[161]

72

Caught up as she was in the life of Greenwich Village, it is not surprising that Latimer became involved in various radical causes and even did some political reporting for *The New Masses*, a radical journal of the twenties. But she was more philosophical than political, and her most intense commitment was to the emerging "Gurdijieff philosophy" which taught that there are three sides to a person: instinctive, mental, and emotional. Exponents of the philosophy practiced an elaborate system of mental and physical exercises through which all three sides were to become fully developed and integrated. Upon moving back to Portage in 1930, Latimer involved Gale in the Gurdijieff movement and soon Portage became a mecca for this philosophical 'cult.' The leader of the cult in the midwest was Jean Toomer, author, lecturer, and 'humanistic psychologist.' A tremendously attractive man, Toomer joined the Portage group in the summer of 1931 to conduct an "experiment in human behavior." Toomer, Latimer, and six other people lived together in a cottage for two months, "breaking their defense crusts," learning to develop their three sides, and trying to "eradicate the false veneer of civilization" so that they could live honestly and happily in a communal situation.[162]

The experiment was quite an event for Portage, Wisconsin in 1931 and the town was abuzz with stories about the mysterious Toomer and his exercises in nude bathing, Tibetan dancing, and tree-climbing. But all gossip subsided at the end of the experiment — which Toomer declared a success — when he and Latimer announced that they would be married at the Portage Episcopal Church on October 30, 1931. Many prominent people attended the wedding, for which Latimer wore a black velvet gown and black velvet turban and carried yellow roses.

Afterward, the Toomers traveled to California to write and lecture and the town of Portage seemed to settle into an acceptance of the now-married Jean Toomer . . . until it was discovered that he was of 'mixed blood,' perhaps one-sixteenth Negro. A streak of racist hatred swept through the town, shaming Latimer's parents, enraging Zona Gale, delighting the Milwaukee and Chicago press. It was the biggest scandal to hit Portage in anyone's memory; to the people of Portage, Margery Latimer was a fallen woman.[163]

We have no record of how Latimer responded to the racism. We know that she adored Toomer, perhaps worshipped him. In a painfully complicated sense, being her husband's disciple may have been the way she resolved her conflicts about love and marriage. Latimer became pregnant soon after she was married and was thrilled at the fulfillment of this dream. "We expect the baby about August 12," she wrote to Gale, "I look forward now to the event with such excitement and such eagerness that all thought of my inadequacy in pain and in life has entirely left me. It seems like my one supreme date with reality."[164]

Margery Latimer died in childbirth on August 17, 1932.

Hildegard Chada

The Depression usually calls to mind soup lines, apple vendors, old cars piled high with belongings headed west, and New York housewives buying week-old bread from the bakery backdoor. The people of northern Wisconsin had none of these luxuries. For them the Depression meant no cars, no lines, no store-bought food; nothing but bare survival, loneliness and isolation. One woman who lived through those years was Hildegard Chada of Boulder Junction in Vilas County.[165]

Chada was a bride of 24 when the stock market crashed. Within two years, she and her husband Orlando had to leave the Schuster Contracting Company in Green Bay and moved to the rural north where they bought eighty acres of tax land. Young and inexperienced, these

brave 'city folk' set about clearing their land to build a three-room house. It was not until the house was built that they realized they would not be able to get water. Chada's daughter, Faith Wyckoff, recalls that "water had to be carried up a long hill from the lake and boiled for drinking . . . If we could not get to the lake, we melted and boiled snow."

Orlando Chada soon got a job at a CCC camp near Star Lake, 25 miles away. This meant that Hildegard Chada was left alone with three small children (and, later, a fourth) for four winters, from 1930 to 1934. The closest neighbor was almost a mile away on the main road and as private roads were not plowed in those days, the Chada family was often snowed in for weeks at a time. Survival was the main occupation; a wood cooking stove had to be tended constantly, water carried, clothes made and mended, meals prepared from the venison and fish kept frozen on the porch, and vegetables canned during the summer. All that Chada canned came from the wilderness since gardens were virtually impossible given the area's climate and the nibblings of local deer and rabbits.

"The adversities of that life are unimagineable now," says Mrs. Wyckoff, "and yet we never felt deprived. Mother made the chores a game in which we all participated . . . She kept us all together for protection and to combat the loneliness and solitude. There was lots of 'let's pretend' and we always sang. She told me as an adult how frightened she was of the wolves and coyotes that howled at night . . . But as children she never gave us a sense of fear of anything."

Life eased somewhat for the Chadas in the years to come, but only because each member of the family worked at all kinds of jobs. "Most everyone was always looking for ways to make money," explains Mrs. Wyckoff. "Even when Mother had no running water or electricity and only a wash board and hand-run wooden washing machine, she did the laundry for the woman who ran the local telephone company. Reforestation of cut-over and burned-over land kept Mr. Chada away from home much of the time, so child-rearing responsibilities prevented Mrs. Chada from taking a job in one of the local resorts. Still, she did devise a scheme for earning money during the tourist season. As soon as their one-car garage was built, the family moved into it and rented their home for the summer. They continued this "business" for several summers, living in the garage on bunk beds and renting their home to a "mystery woman" from Chicago who sketched the area's wildlife . . . but declined to ever reveal her name or address.

Hildegard Chada's pioneer spirit did not diminish with age. During World War II she was inspired by the writings of war correspondent Ernie Pyle and was determined to help in the war effort. She applied for a job superintending the local fire tower since, by 1944, the war had called up all of the area's qualified men. The tower had a radio, so Chada was required to take the Federal Radio License Exam. "She felt very insecure about that," recalls Mrs. Wyckoff, "but we children drilled her every minute we were at home and it was a great triumph for all of us when she passed."

Chada's post at the fire tower was considered "hazardous" because her particular tower had only an outside ladder going 85 feet straight up. According to Mrs. Wyckoff, "it is the only one in the area built that way; the others have stairs that ascend gradually in platforms." Every day for two years, Hildegard Chada walked the two miles from her cabin to the tower, climbed the 85-foot ladder with her daily supplies slung over her shoulder in an onion sack, and settled down to watch for signs of smoke. She had to know the area well enough to distinguish campsite fires from possible forest fires, and she had to be able to calculate exact locations when she radioed for fire-fighting teams.

The fire tower job had no set hours; the weather determined the length of Chada's day. In dry periods she worked until nine or ten o'clock at night. If there was a lightning storm, Chada was 'trapped' in the tower until it passed. If there was a fire she was needed on the radio to report the fire's condition and direction, the density of smoke and wind changes. Often when she worked late, Chada's husband and children carried her dinner up to her and stayed with her during the night vigil.

Hildegard Chada's life was a series of modern pioneer experiences. Her life serves as a reminder that the twentieth century has had its share of women who faced primitive conditions and carried on in a tradition of survival, strength, and ingenuity. Hildegard Chada was one modern pioneer woman who not only survived but contributed to life on the northern Wisconsin frontier.

Emma Toft

"Emma Toft stands as a constant rebuke to unthinking change
. . . She reminds the jaded and fragmented and the harried of what
real people are like . . ."166

On the eastern shore of the Door County peninsula, three miles from
Bailey's Harbor lie 270 acres of virgin timber — the largest stand of
untouched white pine on Wisconsin's Lake Michigan coast. That pine
forest and the 800-acre wildlife sanctuary adjacent to it, owe their existence to the dedication of one woman: Emma Toft.

"Miss Emma," as she is called by the residents of Door County,
has lived among the virgin pine on Toft's Point all her life. Her father,
Thomas Toft, was a native of Denmark but had worked in the pineries
of Michigan and Wisconsin before moving to Bailey's Harbor in 1870 to
work at a limestone quarry in the pine forest. When the quarry was
worked out, Toft bought the property and built a tiny farm there with
his wife and their seven children.167

Emma Toft was born on this land in February of 1891. "In the
home I grew up in," she writes, "I was encouraged to love the land of
Door with all its creatures. My father taught me the trees and wildlife.
My mother knew the flowers."168 As a girl, Emma went on hikes
through the woods with her father and brothers, " as long as I never
let on I was tired and wanted to go home."169

Toft left the forest for a few years to teach school in Wisconsin,
North Dakota and Iowa. By 1917 she had earned enough money to
enter nurses' training at Presbyterian Hospital in Chicago. She was only
there a few months, however, before she had to return home to nurse
her aging parents; and when her father died in 1918, "death kept me
at home with Mother."170

Photo by F.J. Pechman

Toft knew that her parents'
greatest dream was that the
Point be preserved for future
generations. She conceived the
idea of a little family hotel
on the rocky shore where
guests would come for a rest,
good food, and an encounter
with nature. Every summer for
almost 40 years, 'selected
guests' — those people who
loved nature as much as their
host — returned to the Point
to "stay at Toft's Point, eat
her cherry pie, sleep on her
good mattresses in bedsteads
made of saplings lashed together, to wash in the morning
with pitchers and porcelain
basins" — and to look at nature
through Emma Toft's eyes.171

But the hotel guests were not the only people to benefit from Emma Toft's encyclopedic knowledge of plants and wildlife. Countless visitors were guided through her forest — families of campers, groups of college students, conservation clubs, and thousands of Door County school children. All have followed this tall, "regal" woman in her cutoff blue jeans, striding through the forest. "She takes fallen trees and under-brush like a trackman clearing hurdles," wrote one visitor to Toft's Point. "A word here, an explanation there, you realize there aren't many things Emma Toft doesn't know about the plants, shrubs and trees that grow out here on the Point."[172]

Toft lived alone on the Point for over 40 years, but she was never lonely. "I don't see how you can be lonely in your own home," she once said. "All the trees and animals here are my friends." For years the local game warden brought stray baby animals to Toft's door. She would raise the little foxes, birds, fawns and skunks and then give them to the Wildlife Refuge. As a member of the Wisconsin Ornithological Society she used to assist in both the spring and winter bird counts. And as an opponent of open season on deer, she used to stalk her land during deer season, in snow pants and navy peacoat, keeping an eye out for hunters and trespassers.[173]

"Emma Toft is absolutely fearless. She is without fear of animals, solitude, legislation, or mankind."[174]

Despite her legendary devotion to Toft's Point — a devotion which has been tested in numerous lawsuits by hungry developers — Toft is probably best known for her efforts on behalf of the Ridges Sanctuary. The Ridges is Wisconsin's southern-most outpost of boreal forest and the largest preserve of wild flowers in the country. The Ridges began in 1937 when the Door County Park Board slated a 40-acre tract near Bailey's Harbor for development as a trailer park. A public meeting sponsored by the Door County Woman's Club informed local citizens of the value of that tract for conservation purposes. When the bull-dozers moved in to clear the woodland they met a delegation, headed by Emma Toft, who refused to move out of the path. "If you want to go any farther," warned the formidable Toft, "you'll have to scoop us up too." In the end, the Door County Board turned the land over to the people of Bailey's Harbor and they founded the Ridges Sanctuary Corporation to manage and develop it as a wildlife preserve.[175]

A member of the Ridges board of directors since it was founded, Toft has served several terms as president and was for many years its treasurer. She has worked to raise funds for maintaining the sanctuary and for buying additional sanctuary land, and has assisted in the design of trails and tours. Most important, she provided leadership essential to start the Ridges and make it a success. Since 1937 the Ridges has acquired over 700 additional acres of property through purchase and donation, making it the largest corporately-owned flower preserve in the nation.

"We can appreciate through Emma Toft what a sense of wholeness means; we can see what it means to be able to rely upon the sureness and grace which result from such wholeness . . . Her loping stride, both graceful and purposeful, is that of someone who has instinctively preserved her independence . . ."[176]

A few years ago, Toft moved to Bailey's Harbor to live with her sister-in-law during the winter, but three or four times a week she hiked out to her Point on snowshoes to leave food for the animals and check her trees. Now she leaves these winter duties to other local naturalists. But Toft continues to live on Toft's Point in the summers where she is as active as her 85 years will allow. She shies away from publicity, perhaps because she thinks it is foolish to make such a fuss over someone who has simply done what everyone should do, respect and preserve nature. Still, she has received countless awards for her service to the community and her contribution to conservation. She was given the Congressional Medal of Honor in 1964 and has been honored by the State Federation of Women's Clubs, the Milwaukee County Conservation Alliance, the Northeastern Audubon Society, the University of Wisconsin-Green Bay, the Wisconsin Federation of Garden Clubs, and the Door County chapter of the National Organization for Women — to name just a few.

"Emma Toft has, by her own efforts, done what national organizations are now trying to do. She saved a portion of one of the most beautiful parts of America."[177]

There is no danger that Toft's Point will be destroyed when Emma Toft is no longer there to protect it. In 1968 the Toft family sold the Point to Nature Conservancy which, in turn, gave the land to the University of Wisconsin provided that the family be allowed to use the land as long as they lived and that the Point be held as a nature preserve "for scientific, educational, and other esthetic purposes entirely in its natural state."[178]

In 1934 there was a movement for change and reform in Beaver Dam city government. Several of Mary Spellman's former students approached their now-retired math teacher and convinced her to run for mayor on a reform ticket. In a race with three men, including the incumbent, Spellman carried 12 of the city's 14 wards, and in each one had a large majority. She served two terms as Beaver Dam's mayor (1934-38), during which time she was the only woman mayor in Wisconsin and one of the few in the country.[179]

In January, 1943 Rhoda Oshkosh House was appointed judge for the Indian court on the Menominee Reservation. House, the eldest daughter of Menominee Chief Reginald Oshkosh, was the only Indian woman to be appointed to such a post in Wisconsin. As there was no social worker on the reservation at this time, Judge House's duties required that she be a family counselor, welfare worker and children's court counselor as well as the head legal arbiter on the reservation. During her years as judge, House continued to raise the youngest of her 16 children and six of her grandchildren, and continued to serve on the local school board and board of health. This "large and stately woman" served as Menominee judge until the tribe's reservation status was terminated in 1954.[180]

In 1911, the Wisconsin state legislature passed several 'progressive' labor laws and created an Industrial Commission to administer those laws. Among the laws which came under the Commission's supervision were the 'hour laws' for working women and children. In regard to women, these laws specified:

"No female shall be permitted to work in any place of employment for such period or periods of time during any day, night or week, as shall be dangerous or prejudicial to the life, health or safety of such female. It shall be the duty of the Industrial Commission and it shall have the power, jurisdiction and authority, to investigate and determine such reasonable classification, and to issue general or special orders fixing hours of beginning and ending work during any day, night or week which shall be necessary to protect the life, health, safety or welfare of any female. Until such time as the Industrial Commission shall issue general or special orders the following periods of time shall be deemed dangerous or prejudicial to the life or health of females: At daywork, more than 10 hours a day or 55 hours a week, 6 a.m. to 8 p.m. At nightwork, more than 8 hours a night or 48 hours a week, 8 p.m. to 6 a.m."

The statute regarding employment of minors included 40 clauses limiting the number of hours a child between 7 and 16 could work, and specifying the types of employment and times of day in which minors could not be employed. These laws were altered and added to over the years, but one particularly 'revolutionary' addition was the women's minimum wage law passed in 1913.[182]

Recent legal decisions have found 'protective legislation' for women to be discriminatory. But in their day these wage and hour laws were considered major reforms. In 1911 the government and the labor unions were just beginning to assert their power over private industry. Prior to these early controls, industrial conditions were very harmful to employees, particularly to women who were the most exploited, the most 'sweated,' and the least likely to be included in organized labor unions. Working women had so little economic and political leverage that they welcomed protective legislation.

It was not until women's position began to improve and not until labor legislation had advanced to the point where it was possible to demand 'protective legislation' for *all* workers that people could understand the words of one far-sighted feminist of 1912 who declared:

"If women had rights, they wouldn't need protection."[183]

Maud Swett

Maud Swett was present at the creation of the Wisconsin Industrial Commission and saw that Commission grow in stature and authority over a period of 45 years. Swett was 32 when the Commission was created in 1911, and had been working for over a year as a statistician in the Bureau of Labor Statistics. With the reorganization of departments, Swett was promoted to assistant secretary in the new Industrial Commission. Five years later she became a 'field deputy,' inspecting places that employed women and minors, and by 1920 she was the Director of the Woman and Child Labor Department of the Wisconsin Industrial Commission.[184]

This was quite a rapid rise for a woman who is described by all who knew her as "quiet and unassuming," "very modest," "reserved," and even "retiring." Yet all agree that Maud Swett had a way about her, a subtle but impressive dignity that was more powerful than any of the laws she was charged with enforcing. She was, according to former colleague Elizabeth Brandeis Raushenbush, "The ideal public servant: unobstrusive, modest, but absolutely firm as a rock."[185]

As the person in Wisconsin charged with enforcing women's and child labor laws, Swett's main job was to supervise seven women deputies who inspected at every major industrial and commercial enterprise that employed women in Wisconsin. The Woman and Child Labor Department was based in Milwaukee in those days and the department deputies did a great deal of traveling. Swett, herself, continued to make inspections throughout her years with the Commission, particularly where her deputies had found infractions of the law and where employers were resisting compliance. In cases where employers absolutely refused to follow the law, Swett recommended legal proceedings against them, but she had remarkably few situations where such proceedings were necessary. She managed, through a combination of education and firm persuasion, to bring Wisconsin employers in line without alienating them.

This was a time when private employers were still unaccustomed to government regulation — particularly when administered by a woman. But Swett's manner was so direct and so business-like that she soon won the respect and cooperation of almost every employer she met.

Maud Swett was responsible for enforcing legislation, not developing it and she was "very meticulous" about her role in legislative hearings. She felt it was inappropriate for a public employee to lobby but she did provide technical advice to those who wished to draft labor legislation for women and children. Over the years she worked closely with Wisconsin's leaders in labor law, John R. Commons, Selig Perlman, and E.B. Raushenbush. In 1919, Swett advised Commons on raising women's minimum wage, arguing that the minimum wage *should* be raised but only moderately. Swett believed that if the new minimum was set too high, women would be fired. Swett also assisted in the re-drafting of the Child Labor Law in 1937. Since passage in 1911, the law had become a jumble of administrative codes tacked on year after year to suit changing conditions. Swett and E.B. Raushenbush recodified the "very messy" law, making it more understandable and much easier to enforce.[186]

Administration was really Swett's forte, and yet her niece, Gladys Trayser of Madison, recalls that "she was not naturally efficient."[187] Instead, she was an incomparable supervisor and thus developed an extremely efficient, devoted staff. Her secretary for over 25 years, Evelyn Doyle, wrote recently that this "Great lady was admired and respected" by all those under her. "She was never too busy to help them with their problems, personal or otherwise." Not only did Swett have "unlimited capacity for enforcing legislation for the betterment of women," explains Doyle, "she was helpful to people from other countries who came to her for advice and help."[188] In the course of her career, Swett trained 18 visitors from 12 foreign countries in the enforcement of labor laws. These trainees were sent to her by the U.S. Department of Labor where it was felt that Swett's example was "outstanding in the whole United States." Her papers include numerous letters of thanks from foreign students who trained under her, as well as from young women who began their labor work in Wisconsin and went on to introduce Swett's techniques in other states.[189]

Throughout 30 of her 45 years with the state, Swett's office was located in Milwaukee and she kept an apartment in that city. But in 1926 she bought a house on Roby Road in Madison which she shared with her mother, sister, and her niece and nephews. Later, she shared the home with her niece, her niece's husband, and their four children. Swett returned to this home every weekend for 30 years. "She had a hand in raising me and my brothers," says Trayser, "and also in raising my four children — she was an important influence in their lives. My brothers and I and my own children had the advantage of living in an extended family and my aunt was a vital part of it."[190]

Swett's life in Milwaukee was as full as her life in Madison, for she was active in numerous organizations — particularly the Y.W.C.A., the City Club, the County League of Women Voters and the Milwaukee Legal Aid Society. In 1947 she was the first recipient of the Milwaukee County League's Caroline Bigelow McGeoch award for distinguished citizenship.

Swett retired at the age of 77. "She waited too long to retire," says her niece. "But she wanted to finish compiling some material and was determined to stay as long as they wanted her — and they wanted her as long as she would stay!" When she did retire in 1956, letters poured in from labor officials all over the country and from employers all over the state, testifying to the many different services she performed and thanking her for always being "fair." Though strict about accepting gifts during her administration, Swett did accept a Wagner carpet sweeper upon retirement "as a symbol of women's work." According to the accompanying letter, "The sweeper was welded, painted, packed and assembled by women. . .and should it ever need repair, it would be a woman who would analyze the problem and make the adjustment." No one knows whatever became of that carpet sweeper but it must have pleased Swett to receive it as a token of her efforts to "assure women of this state the opportunity to work under adequate conditions with a fair return for their effort."[191]

Alma Kuhn

Alma Kuhn was a community leader and one-woman dynamo in Wisconsin's Washington County from the 1940's through the 1960's. Best known by her neighbors as the organizer and director of the local 4-H, Kuhn was equally active as a farm wife, mother of five and participant in numerous service organizations.[192]

When Kuhn started working with the Oak Grove 4-H in 1937 — "just to help with some cooking and sewing projects" — it was made up of 20 to 30 boys and girls from the farms in the Rockfield-Richfield area. When Kuhn died in 1970, the club had almost seventy members, many of them from town, and had expanded its program to include photography, electricity, houseplants, and exploring along with such standard 4-H classes as cooking, sewing, dairying, woodworking and crafts.

Kuhn's record as a 4-H leader suggests that she cared more about participation than productivity. She worked to involve each member in some sort of project that would give him or her a sense of worth and accomplishment. For Kuhn, this meant individual instruction, two to three special project meetings each Saturday around her kitchen table, careful record-keeping so she knew each child's progress, individual meetings with parents, finding and supervising other adult project leaders, committee meetings to plan programs, and organizing the 4-H 'demonstrations' for county and state fairs, as well as for a local Oak Grove Fair which Kuhn established for those 4-H'ers who did not get to exhibit at the larger fair.

In addition to her work with the 4-H, Kuhn served on the Washington County Library Committee and was chair of the Germantown Library Board; was a charter member, ofttime president and historian of the Rockfield Homemaker's Club; was a member of the Cedar Lake Home Auxiliary, a church retirement and nursing home which she visited once a week to mend clothes, iron, and 'help out'; taught Sunday School every Sunday for 15 years; was active in the church Women's Guild as an officer, program planner, m.c., and cook for all Guild functions; was a member of Eastern Star; was active in planning Rockfield's annual 'Hi-Neighbor' party; and as a 4-H leader concerned with health, she conducted surveys in the community to test the drinking water and check for fire hazards.

During World War II she organized the Oak Grove 4-H into a volunteer force which collected everything from scrap metal to milk weed pods (for use in making life preservers). Kuhn supervised this activity while she herself was working at the Red Cross rolling bandages and helping her husband with the Kuhn's farm and gravel business. The gravel business boomed during the war and Alma Kuhn worked on it at home, taking all the orders, dispatching the drivers and fielding complaints.

The Kuhns were not wealthy but their years of hard work had made them comfortable. Alma Kuhn could have afforded to escape household chores. She chose not to — for a whole host of reasons; because she enjoyed the household arts, because it was a way for this busy woman to tell her family she loved them, because women in her community simply did these things without question, and probably because Kuhn's energy and background prevented her from ever limiting her load.

The eldest daughter in a German Lutheran family, Alma Gutknecht was born in 1896 and raised on a farm on Lake Michigan in Sheboygan County. She was raised to work hard but soon learned that if she wanted to do more than farm work, she would have to strike out on her own. She left home at age 14, against her parents' wishes, to attend high school in Sheboygan where, for the first time in her life, she was expected to speak only English. Upon graduation in 1915, she attended Oshkosh State Normal School and graduated in 1917 at age 21. She had supported herself through all these years of school with a series of unpleasant jobs waiting tables, washing dishes, and babysitting. As a teacher at Oak Grove School in Rockfield, she lived with the Kuhn family and met their son William. The Kuhns married in 1922 but Alma Kuhn continued to teach school until the birth of her first child in 1923. The next four children came in 1926, 1928, 1930 and 1932.

The Kuhn children grew up in a home full of activity. In addition to all her community work, Alma Kuhn was an avid gardener. She had plants and flowers everywhere, including a large collection of African violets. She kept a garden every year in which she planted all types of vegetables and flowers. She also grew strawberries, raspberries, gooseberries, currants, cherries, plums, pears and apples and canned gallons of fruits, vegetables and jams every summer. And every Saturday — regardless of how many 4-H meetings were being held in her kitchen — Alma Kuhn baked. Every Saturday she turned out breads, rolls, coffeecakes, kuchens, and pies. And every Sunday for many years — after teaching Sunday School and attending church — Kuhn served Sunday dinner to her husband's family. Sometimes this meant 12 to 20 guests. As a mother and a grandmother, Kuhn sewed beautiful clothes, mended everything, darned socks, and would needlepoint, knit, embroider, quilt, weave or crochet whatever fell into her lap.

Despite her perpetual motion, Kuhn was close to her children and to her grandchildren and worked hard at keeping communications open through the years. When she was in her 70's, Kuhn wrote by hand a 200-page memoir of her childhood on the farm and life in the early 1900's. She presented this memoir, along with her own illustrations, to her granddaughter for her 16th birthday. In closing the memoir Kuhn wrote:

"There have been remarkable changes in work, social life, entertainment, and political life in the last 50 years. I was one who saw the difference. There have been great improvements in everything we see and do. Enjoy yourself."

Esther Streiff Stauffacher

The Swiss community of New Glarus in Green County is renowned for its efforts to preserve Swiss heritage and customs. The public is acquainted with these efforts through the annual Wilhelm Tell Pageant and the New Glarus Historical Museum — two major undertakings which owe their existence to Esther Strieff Stauffacher, a New Glarus native who "lived more in her 43 years than most of us do in twice that long."193

Born in 1902, the daughter of a blacksmith, Esther Strieff was educated through high school in New Glarus. She married Werner Stauffacher when she was 18 and set up housekeeping on their dairy farm just outside New Glarus. As a 'typical' New Glarus farm wife in the 1920's, Stauffacher participated in the 'typical' community activities; she was active in the Swiss Evangelical and Reformed Church, served as president of both the Ladies' Aid Society and the Women's Missionary Society, and joined with her neighbors in the Ladies' "Germania" Society. But Stauffacher brought to all these 'typical' activities a unique gift: a lovely, full contralto voice and the ability to "sit down and make a piano talk." In a community like New Glarus where tradition and fellowship are particularly prized, Esther Stauffacher's musical talents were well-love and well-used. She and her sister, Doris Ott, sang for every funeral, wedding, and church service held in the community; she was the director of every choral group, including the prize-winning New Glarus 4-H chorus and the New Glarus Yodlers; and was a part of the entertainment at most parties and gatherings.

Because Stauffacher was a cultural leader in the community, it was natural for Edwin Barlow to contact her first when he thought about staging a folkfest in New Glarus using Wilhelm Tell as the central theme. Barlow was New Glarus' most wealthy and most worldly citizen. A bit eccentric, he was nonetheless devoted to the small Swiss settlement and contributed a great deal to it, both materially and spiritually. Barlow liked Stauffacher and respected her judgement. It was she who spearheaded the drive to stage the first folkfest/pageant in 1938 and she who helped nurse it to success as a major community event in Wisconsin. She also played a role in the all-amateur pageant from 1938 until her early death in 1945.

The activity surrounding the first production of "Wilhelm Tell" sparked the New Glarus community into establishing a small museum for displaying Swiss artifacts and items from New Glarus history. Stauffacher was serving at the time as president of the Green County Historical Society and soon found herself functioning as the caretaker of the Historical Cabin in New Glarus. The cabin still stands on the New Glarus Historic Restoration site, but it is now only one of many buildings that contain articles and information on New Glarus history. In Stauffacher's day, the cabin was all there was and it was crammed full' of artifacts and memorabilia, some of which were quite valuable. . . but none of which could be properly displayed in such small quarters. Still, Esther Stauffacher spent every Saturday and Sunday afternoons at the cabin, explaining the displays to visitors, answering questions, and passing on folktales and stories about Swiss culture. She was never paid for this work but those who run the museum today credit her as its founder and guiding spirit.

Eleanor Raasch Friedrick

"Women had a real job telling union men that we were here to stay," says Eleanor Raasch Friedrick, 20-year veteran and founding member of the Bakery and Confectionary Workers' International Union in Milwaukee. Friedrick would know, for she was one of the few women to penetrate the leadership ranks of Wisconsin's labor unions in the 1930's and '40's. From the organization of the Confectionary Workers' Local 244 in 1935 until her retirement in 1959, Friedrick was the union's salaried business representative, one of the only women in Wisconsin who actually sat at the bargaining table and negotiated every contract the union made.[194]

Like most union workers in the early days, Friedrick did not set out to be a labor organizer; it was just something that happened. In fact, young Eleanor Olsen was not particularly labor conscious when she went to work for the National Biscuit Company in 1919. Even though her Danish father was in the glassblowers' union in Milwaukee and her mother was in the Women's Auxiliary, Eleanor was not terribly concerned about unionization, nor did she feel particularly oppressed working at a non-union plant like National Biscuit. In time she was promoted to supervisor on her floor and then to pay clerk. All seemed to be going well, though there was some discontent among the 75 per cent female workforce at National when the management ruled that women married after December 31, 1931 would be fired. Eleanor Olsen had become Eleanor Raasch in October, 1931 so she "made it just under the wire," but she can remember some friends who were fired and more who lied about their marital status.

It took time for the workers to realize that they did not have to succumb to every whim of the management. "In those days, your boss could fire you if your hair was parted wrong," explains Friedrick. But in 1934 the workers at National biscuit began to organize and in response to their organizing activities the management called a lock-out for July 4, 1934. The fight was on and Friedrick suddenly found herself with a new job. "I was made picket captain because I'd been pay clerk so I knew everyone's right name, not just the nicknames." It took several months, but the union finally established itself at National Biscuit and Friedrick had yet another job: business representative for the Confectionary Workers' Local 244.

Both the union and its business representative had a great deal to learn if they were to work effectively for the membership. But a review of Friedrick's record shows that she learned quickly and served well during her 24 years with Local 244. Looking at some of her achievements reminds us what workers — particularly women workers — were up against. Once the union could bargain, the rule against married women was struck down, as was the rule that married women and then single women would be laid off before men. It was considered a major victory when the union negotiated for elevators for the multi-storied plant to save workers' time during their half-hour lunch break; and it was no less a victory when the union got 15 minutes 'uniform pay' to cover the time workers had to spend putting on and taking off their work clothes.

These may seem like small concerns, but they had a significant affect on the quality of working conditions at National Biscuit and each small concession required just as much tact and firmness at the bargaining table as did the major issues like workmen's compensation and unemployment insurance. As business agent for Local 244, Eleanor Raasch Friedrick saw all these provisions implemented and saw the union movement become firmly established in the Milwaukee industrial scene. She even saw the "Union Business Agents' Luncheon Club" sexually integrated, "but it took me two years to get in because I didn't wear pants!"

Friedrick was widowed in the 1950's. Today she lives in Milwaukee with her second husband, Jacob Friedrick. She continues to support the efforts of women to attain leadership roles in the labor unions and is optimistic about working women's progress. Friedrick thinks it took Wisconsin women a long time to become union-oriented because for so many years they worked only part-time and viewed their working lives as being short-term. Today, however, Wisconsin women know that — married or not — they will be employed for a good many years.

Eleanor Raasch   Friedrick credits a large part of her education in labor politics to Maud Leonard McCreery a fiery newspaper reporter, Socialist, labor activist, and lecturer who lived in Milwaukee in the 1930's.[195]

Maud Leonard grew up in Wauwautosa in the 1880's, the daughter of a veterinarian. She married Rex McCreery in the early 1900's and began to emerge as a public figure during the peak years of the suffrage campaign, 1912-1920, when she was known as a dynamic organizer and speaker. Her reputation as an activist grew when she went on a nation-wide tour with the League to Enforce the Peace before the U.S. entry into World War I. Separated from her husband in 1919, McCreery went to work as publicity director for the Wisconsin Anti-Tuberculosis Association, but her big break came when she was hired as the woman's editor on Victor Berger's Socialist newspaper The Milwaukee Leader *in the late twenties. Soon, McCreery was the representative of the newswriters' local No. 9 to the Milwaukee Federated Trades Council, a coalition of trade unions in the Milwaukee area.*

It was through her association with the Council that McCreery was able to reach other women in the Milwaukee labor movement. She organized Auxiliaries for workers' wives, encouraging them to be informed and involved in their husbands' unions; and she tried to organize traditionally union-shy women workers, such as the clericals at the Northwest Mutual Life Insurance Company. But her most important contribution was to the education of union members like Eleanor Raasch Friedrick who were anxious to learn and in a position to put their knowledge into action.

Around 1937, McCreery began teaching classes for women at the Milwaukee Labor College. The class content included parliamentary law, public speaking, drawing up contracts, and conducting negotiations. But the real purpose of the classes, says former student Eleanor Friedrick, was "to teach working girls to speak for themselves. . . Women in unions were pushed to the side until Maud McCreery taught us to stand on our." McCreery's motto was "Organize, Agitate, and Educate." She knew that women would have to adopt this motto if they were ever to take control of their working lives and she devoted herself to helping women realize their own rights and power as workers and union members.

Wisconsin and the Federal Equal Rights Amendment

> "How would you, Mrs. Wife, like to discover some morning that your husband had willed away your children, or that you couldn't sue for personal injury damages unless your husband consented and joined you? Seem like silly questions, but such things are possible in these United States. And what brings the subject up now is that Uncle Sam is likely to do something about it in the near future. The federal equal rights amendment has a good chance of going through the next session of Congress."
>
> —Mabel Raef Putnam, The Wisconsin State Journal, *November, 1939.*[196]

Mabel E. Griswold was the president and founder of the Wisconsin Society for the Equal Rights Amendment. Griswold was active in the National Woman's Party and founded the Wisconsin Society in 1947. Under her leadership the Society engaged in lobbying and public education throughout Wisconsin. With Griswold's death in 1955, the Society became inactive and disbanded.[197]

> "It is a national shame that in this supposedly enlightened age so much of the time and energy of publicly spirited women should have to be devoted to obtaining rights that should be theirs as citizens. . . We refer, of course, to the struggle for the adoption of the equal rights amendment to the Constitution of the United States. This amendment was first introduced into Congress in 1923. . .The amendment has been in and out of Congress ever since then. . . Both the Democratic and Republican parties pledged their support to the amendment in the 1944 platforms. . .The stalling on this issue when so much has been promised and when realization of the goals is so imminent is a disgrace. . ."
>
> Editorial, *The Capitol Times,* July 12, 1947.[198]

Footnotes

1   Kohler, Ruth DeYoung. *The Story of Wisconsin Women.* The Committee on Wisconsin Women for the 1948 Wisconsin Centennial, p. 8.

2   Christensen, Rosemary Ackley. "Indian Women: A Historical and Personal Perspective." Paper presented to Second Annual Conference on Minority Studies, April, 1974, University of Wisconsin — LaCrosse.

3   Scanlan, Peter L. "Crawford County Practitioners, 1814-1896." Paper on file in the Manuscripts Division, Wisconsin State Historical Society, Madison. (Hereafter referred to as: Mss. Div, WSHS).

4   Information on Electa Quinney was located in the files of the Stockbridge-Munsee Reservation museum with the aid of Beatrice Miller, museum curator.

5   The Honorable E.S. Miner of Necedah. Quoted in *Muh-He-Ha-Ne-Ok: A History of the Stockbridge Nation* by John Nelson Davidson. Milwaukee: 1893, p. 56.

6   "Early Wisconsin Teachers," *Wisconsin Journal of Education,* December, 1891. Article on file at WSHS.

7   Baker, Charles M. "Pioneer History of Walworth County." In *Wisconsin Historical Society Collections, 1869-72,* vol. 6, pp. 436-475.

8   Hilgen, Katherine Louise. "German Pioneer Letters," *The Wisconsin Magazine of History,* 16 (June, 1933), 437.

      The Wisconsin Magazine of History is published and copyrighted by the State Historical Society of Wisconsin, Madison, Wisconsin.

9   Information on the Pratt family was located in the Mss. Div., WSHS. In addition to the diary kept by Sarah Pratt, there is a brief memoir by Susannah Pratt and a family history, written in 1931, by a descendant, Edith Hadley, of Janesville.

10   Sproat, Florantha Thompson. "LaPointe Letters," *The Wisconsin Magazine of History,* 16 (December, 1932), 199.

11   Bale, Florence Gratiot. "A Packet of Old Letters," *The Wisconsin Magazine of History,* vol. 11, pp. 159-163.

12   "First Wisconsin School Opened in June, 1829 by Kin of Madison Woman." Located in the Newspaper Clipping Scrapbook on file at the Madison Public Library, pamphlet file.

13   Bale, op. cit.

14   Information on Marion Johnson Cooper was provided by her great-grandson, William Cooper of Wauwautosa, Wisconsin. Mr. Cooper has done extensive research on his family's history; his 12-page biography of Marion Johnson Cooper supplied the data for this sketch.

15   "Negro Suffrage and Woman's Rights in the Convention of 1846," *The Wisconsin Magazine of History,* 3 (December, 1919), 227-230.

16   Nesbit, Robert C. *Wisconsin: A History.* Madison: The University of Wisconsin Press; 1973, pp. 218-220.

17   Information on Mariette Huntly Snell was derived from an interview with Mrs. Hannah Swart, curator of the Hoard Museum in Fort Atkinson, and from materials on file at the Hoard Museum.

18   "Genealogy of the Snells," *Jefferson County Union,* December 12, 1924.

19   Purucker, Mrs. George. "The Snell Family." Paper presented to the Fort Atkinson Tuesday Club, April 27, 1971.

20   Gattiker, Emma. "Some Notes on Early Swiss Settlers in Sauk County — Honey Creek Township." Paper on file in the Mss. Div, WSHS.

21 Weisensel, Peter Roy. "The Wisconsin Temperance Crusade to 1919." Masters Thesis, University of Wisconsin — Madison, 1965.

22 Information on Emma Brown was located at the Hoard Museum in Fort Atkinson. The Museum has a set of the *Wisconsin Chief* dating from 1860 to 1889. The Museum also has Brown's obituary which provided information on her work with the Good Templars.

23 "Women as Journalists: Some Women Who Conduct Successful Papers in Wisconsin," *The Milwaukee Sentinel*, March 15, 1891.

24 Information on the Kumliens was derived primarily from a three-part biography by granddaughter Angie Kumlien Main for the *Wisconsin Magazine of History*, vol. 27, September and December, 1943, March, 1944.

25 Main, A.K. Ibid, pp. 198-208.

26 Bjoraker, Walter. T. "Thure Kumlien, Koshkonong Naturalist." Paper presented before the Ygdrasii Society, January 8, 1972, on file at the Hoard Museum, Fort Atkinson.

27 Baer, Marcie. "In Recognition of Womanhood: Their Role in Manitowoc County History," *The Manitowoc County Historical Society Newsletter*, September, 1973.

28 Nesbit, Robert C., op. cit., p. 248.

29 Duckett, Kenneth A. "Ella Hobart: Wisconsin's Woman Chaplain of the Civil War," *30th Star*, 2 (December, 1956) 1-2.

30 "Eliza T. Wilson," pamphlet on file at WSHS.

31 Curtiss-Wedge, F., Jones, George O., et. al., compilers. *History of Dunn County*. Minneapolis: H.C. Cooper Jr. and Company, 1925. p. 833-834.

32 Wroolie, Mrs. T.S.V. "An Immigrant's Memories," *The Wisconsin Magazine of History*, vol. 30, p. 439.

33 Hurn, Ethel Alice. *Wisconsin Women in the War Between the States*. Madison: Wisconsin History Commission, Original Papers, No. 6, May, 1911.

34 Mary Schaal John's complete story is on file in the Mss. Div., WSHS.

35 Nesbit, Robert., op. cit., p. 258.

36 Merk, Frederick. *Economic History of Wisconsin During the Civil War Decade*. Madison: The State Historical Society of Wisconsin; 1916, p. 167.

37 Information on Letitia Abbott Wall was located in "Letitia Wall, A Wisconsin Pioneer Type," by Joseph Schafer, *The Wisconsin Magazine of History*, vol. 8, pp. 193-198.

38 Hurn, Ethel Alice., op. cit., p. 85.

39 Information on Ann Bicknell Ellis was located at the Hoard Museum in Fort Atkinson.

40 Information on the progress of women at U.W. was located in "Coeducation at the Wisconsin State University," by Helen R. Olin, pamphlet on file at the WSHS. *Higher Education in Wisconsin* by William F. Allen and David E. Spencer, Washington: Government Printing Office, 1889, pp. 37-41. *The University of Wisconsin: A History, 1848-1925, Vol. I*, by Merle Curti and Vernon Carstensen, Madison: University of Wisconsin Press, 1949.

41 Mrs. Edna Phillips Chynoweth's recollections of student life at the University of Wisconsin are on file in the Mss. Div., WSHS.

42 Bascom, Florence. "The University in 1874-1887," *The Wisconsin Magazine of History*, vol. 8, p. 306.

43 Information on Clarissa Tucker Tracy was located in *The Life and Poems of Clarissa Tucker Tracy* by Ada C. Merrell. Chicago: 1908.

44   Pernin, Rev. Peter. "The Great Peshtigo Fire: An Eyewitness Account," William Converse Haygood, editor, *The Wisconsin Magazine of History*, 54 (Summer, 1971), 271.

45   Information on Elizabeth Robinson Stone was supplied by her granddaughter, Irene Learned Christiansen, of Storm Lake, Iowa. Several of Mrs. Christiansen's observations about her grandmother are quoted in the sketch.

46   Phillips, Dennis H. "Women in Nineteenth Century Wisconsin Medicine." Paper prepared for graduate seminar in history at U.W.-Madison, 1973.

47   Information on Betsy Thunder was derived from an interview with her granddaughter Flora Thundercloud Bearheart, of Tomah, Wisconsin; and with Frances Perry of Black River Falls, Wisconsin, on February 20, 1975.

48   *Reports of Cases Argued and Determined in the Supreme Court of the State of Wisconsin*, v. 39, p. 232.

49   Berryman, John R. *The History of the Bench and Bar of Wisconsin*. Chicago: H.C. Cooper, Jr. and Company, 1898. v. 2, p. 501. *Report of the Proceedings of the Wisconsin State Bar Association, Biographical Sketches, 1878-1885*. p. 249.

50   *Reports of Cases Argued and Determined in the Supreme Court of the State of Wisconsin*, op. cit., pp. 235-238.

51   Ibid, p. 240.

52   Ibid, pp. 242-243.

53   Ibid, pp. 244-245.

54   Drews, Dora M. "For Women, A Slow Climb," *The Wisconsin State Journal*, June 18, 1950.

55   Berryman, op. cit., v. 1. Gores, Stan. "Kate Pier, Three Daughters All Earned Law Degrees," *The Fond du Lac Commonwealth-Reporter*, June 10, 1966.

56   Clark, James I. "Wisconsin Women Fight for Suffrage." Pamphlet published by the State Historical Society of Wisconsin, 1956. p.7.

57   Ibid, pp. 5-6.

58   Graves, Lawrence. "The Wisconsin Woman Suffrage Movement." Ph.D. dissertation, University of Wisconsin-Madison, 1954.

59   Clark, op. cit., p. 5.

60   Pamphlet file, "The Wisconsin Woman Suffrage Movement," WSHS.

61   Whyte, Bertha Kitchell. *Our Wisconsin Heritage*. Newton, Massachusetts: Charles T. Branford Company, 1954. pp. 231-245.

62   Ibid, p. 237.

63   Grant, Pauline. "Pauline Jacobus: Her Art Pottery Was Famous," *Wisconsin Then and Now*, 21 (August, 1974), 6.

64   Whyte, op. cit., p. 240.

65   Grant, op. cit.

66   Mariner, Mary A. "The Woman's Club of Milwaukee, 1876-1923." Pamphlet on file, WSHS.

67   "America's Only Woman Bookmaker," *The Sunday Sentinel* (Milwaukee), November 12, 1899. Newspaper articles on Helen Bruneau VanVechten are on file in the Mss. Div., WSHS.

68   Wallin, Florence. "Influences Explaining the Course and Development of the Philosopher Press in Wausau, Wisconsin," Master's thesis, Wayne State University, 1968. Ms. Wallin is Helen Bruneau VanVechten's grand-niece.

69   *The Sunday Sentinel*, op. cit.

70   "A Woman Book Publisher," *The St. Louis Globe-Democrat*, February 5, 1899. Wallin, op. cit.

71   *The Sunday Sentinel*, op. cit.

72   Letter from Mrs. A.M. Evans of Wausau, Wisconsin. Mrs. Evans is Helen Bruneau VanVechten's niece.

73   Wallin, op. cit.

74   Clark, op. cit., pp. 7-8.

75   Mrs. B.H. Strong's eulogy to Ida Wright Albers in on file in the Hannah Taggert Patchin Papers, Mss. Div., WSHS.

76   Smith, Mary Miller. *Memories of Long Ago: The Autobiography of a Baptist Preacher's Wife.* Los Angeles: 1935.

77   "Milwaukee Business and Professional Women," *The Free Press,* 1904. Article on file in the Women's Resource Center, Alverno College, Milwaukee.

78   Editorial copied by Clara Bewick Colby was copied, by hand, into Hannah Taggert Patchin's scrapbook, on file in the Mss. Div., WSHS.

79   Brown, Rev. Olympia. *Democratic Ideals — A Sketch of Clara Bewick Colby.* New York: The Federal Suffrage Association, 1917.

80   Chase, Mary Ellen. *A Goodly Fellowship.* New York: Macmillan Co., 1940. p.117.

81   Ibid, p. 91.

82   Wright, Frank Lloyd. *Frank Lloyd Wright: An Autobiography.* New York: Duell, Sloan, and Pearce, 1943. pp. 132-137.

83   Ibid

84   Letters documenting the Lloyd-Jones' dispute over Hillside Home School are on file in the Mss. Div., WSHS.

85   "Suffrage Society Elects Officers," *The Wisconsin State Journal,* January 8, 1917.

86   Porritt, Annie G. *Laws Affecting Women and Children in the Suffrage and Non-Suffrage States.* New York: National Woman Suffrage Publishing Co., Inc., 1917. p. 102.

87   Lesy, Michael. *Wisconsin Death Trip.* New York: Pantheon Books, 1973.

88   Waligorski, Ann Shirley. "Social Action and Women: The Experience of Lizzie Black Kander." Master's thesis, University of Wisconsin-Madison, 1970. Ms. Waligorski's thesis was the main source of information for this sketch.

89   Levin, Alexandra Lee. "The Jastrows in Madison: A Chronicle of University Life, 1888-1900." *The Wisconsin Magazine of History,* 46 (Summer, 1963), 243-256.

90   Swarsensky, M. *From Generation to Generation: The Story of the Madison Jewish Community.* Madison: 1955. pp. 77-78.

91   "Careers of Lawrence College Co-eds," *The Lawrentian,* May 31, 1916.

92   Curtis, Wardon A. "The Movement Against Co-education at the University of Wisconsin," *The Independent,* 65 (August, 6, 1908), 326.

93   Heath, Frederick. "The Typewriter in Wisconsin," *The Wisconsin Magazine of History,* 27 (March, 1944), 272.

94   Holmes, Fred J. *Wisconsin, v. III.* Chicago: The Lewis Publishing Company, 1946. p. 260.

95   "Women Employees in the State Capitol," *The Milwaukee Sentinel,* April 1, 1900.

96   Kubista, Harriet. Article in *The Wisconsin State Employee,* April, 1935. The article on Mary Derenzo was made available by Ms. Kubista who opened her clipping files to the project staff.

97   Stearns, Lutie. "My First Seventy-Five Years: Part I, 1866-1914." *The Wisconsin Magazine of History,* 42 (Spring, 1959) 216.

98   Tannenbaum, Earl. "The Library Career of Lutie Eugenia Stearns," *The Wisconsin Magazine of History,* 39 (Spring, 1956) 161.

99   Harris, Adelaide Evans. "Books That Travel: Any Books — For Anybody — By Mail Prepaid: A Promise to Obtain Anything Available in Print for the People of Wisconsin," *The World's Work,* 49 (March, 1925) 551.

100   Ibid

101   Stearns, Lutie. "My First Seventy-Five Years: Part II, 1914-1925." *The Wisconsin Magazine of History,* 42 (Summer, 1959) 282-287. And, "Part III: Increasingly Personal," 43 (Winter, 1959-60) 97.

102   Ibid, Part III, p.101.

103   Ibid, Part II, p.283.

104   Ibid, Part III, p. 98.

105 Ibid

106 Ibid, p. 100.

107 Ibid, p. 97.

108 Duckett, Kenneth A. "Suffragettes on the Stump: Letter from the Political Equality League of Wisconsin, 1912," *The Wisconsin Magazine of History*, 38 (Autumn, 1954) 31.

109 Youmans, Theodora W. "How Wisconsin Women Won the Ballot," *The Wisconsin Magazine of History*, 5 (1921-22) 3-32.

110 Duckett, op. cit., pp. 31-32.

111 All Items from *The Wisconsin Citizen* are located in the single bound volume of that journal on file at the WSHS.

112 Frooman, Jack. "The Wisconsin Peace Movement, 1915-1919." Ph.D. dissertation, University of Wisconsin-Madison, 1949. p. 49.

113 Kellogg, Louise P. "Brief Sketch of the Life and Work of Julia Grace Wales," 1915. On file in the Julia Grace Wales Papers, Mss. Div. WSHS.

114 Trattner, Walter I. "Julia Grace Wales and the Wisconsin Plan for Peace," *The Wisconsin Magazine of History*, 44 (Spring, 1961) 205.

115 A scrapbook of newspaper clippings on Wales is on file in the Julia Grace Wales Papers, Mss. Div., WSHS. The file also includes biographical sketches of Wales and her letters.

116 Ibid

117 "Wisconsin Peace Plan to Hague," *The Wisconsin State Journal*, April 8, 1915.

118 The papers of the Women's International League for Peace and Freedom are on file in the Mss. Div., WSHS.

119 Youmans, Theodora W. Editorial in *The Wisconsin Citizen*, January, 1917.

120 Still, Bayrd. *Milwaukee, The History of a City*. Madison: State Historical Society of Wisconsin, 1948.

121 "The Wisconsin People's History Calendar, 1974," The Wisconsin Alliance, Madison, 1973.

122 Youmans, Theodora W. Editorial in *The Wisconsin Citizen*, March, 1915.

123 Putnam, Mabel Raef. *The Winning of the First Bill of Rights for American Women*. Milwaukee: 1924.

124 A reprint of the newspaper article announcing the passage of the Wisconsin Equal Rights Law is to be found in Putnam, op.'cit., pp. 65-66.

125 Gale, Zona. "Is Wisconsin's Equal Rights Law Proving Beneficial to Women? Pro," *The Congressional Digest;* March, 1924, p. 205.

126 Turner, Jennie McMullin and Hochstein, Irma. "Is Wisconsin's Equal Rights Law Proving Beneficial to Women? Con," *The Congressional Digest;* March, 1924, p. 205.

127 Briggs, Michael. "The Wisconsin Equal Rights Statute." Unpublished paper made available through the Governor's Commission on the Status of Women.

128 All information on Margaret Porter Radcliffe was provided by her granddaughter, Margaret Jane Park, President of the West Allis Historical Society. Ms. Park is currently working on a biography of her grandmother and has kept extensive files and scrapbooks documenting her life.

129 All information on Ida Pope Ehle was provided by her daughter, Marguerite Ehle Ellsworth, of Milwaukee. Some of Mrs. Ellsworth's observations about her mother are quoted in the sketch.

130 Engen, Susan. "Grace Pilgrim Bloom: An American Woman," paper prepared for a history course at U.W.-LaCrosse, 1973. p. 6.

131 All information on Sr. Mary Victoria was provided by Sr. Marian Voelker, historian, Congregation of the Third Order of St. Francis of Mary Immaculate, Joliet, Illinois. Sr. Mary Victoria was suggested for the project by Delores Bainbridge of Bayfield, Wisconsin.

132 All information on Marie Francek Illichman was provided by her daughter, Blanche Illichmann Mendl, of Deerbrook, Wisconsin. Some of Mrs. Mendl's reminiscences about her mother are quoted in the sketch.

133 Arenz, Katherine Ann. "Elizabeth Comstock: The Doctor and the Woman," paper prepared for a history course at U.W.-LaCrosse, 1973. p. 9.
134 Rogow, Sally. "Indian Doctor: Rose Minoka Hill, M.D." Copyright August, 1969, Ottawa, Canada. On file in the Mss. Div., WSHS.
135 Essential information about Dr. Hill was supplied by her son, Norbert Hill, Sr. of Oneida, and her grandsons, Norbert Jr. and Charles. The Hill family also provided two newspaper articles about Dr. Hill's career and awards.
136 Interview by Ms. Phyllis Sander with Mrs. Lucille Jonjak of Hayward, Wisconsin, on April 1, 1975. Mrs. Jonjak originally suggested Mrs. Potter for inclusion in this project. All information on Mrs. Potter was collected by Ms. Sander, public librarian in Exeland, Wisconsin. Ms. Sander recorded and transcribed six hours of interviews with Mrs. Potter's friends and relatives for use in this project.
137 Interview with Alma Grimh and Tina Edberg of Radisson, April 23, 1975.
138 Interview with Harriet Solberg, of Exeland, April 17, 1975.
139 Interviews with Alma Grimh and Tina Edberg; and with Mrs. Potter's grandson, Willard Villiard of Radisson, April 12, 1975.
140 Interview with Willard Villiard.
141 Interview with Alma Grimh and Tina Edberg.
142 Interview with Coral Waite of Exeland, April 21, 1975.
143 Letter to Phyllis Sander from Clayton Rutherford of Coolidge, Arizona, April 30, 1975.
144 Interview with Alma Grimh.
145 Interview with Willard Villiard.
146 Letter from Clayton Rutherford.
147 Interview with Ms. Eulalia Croll in Miwaukee, April 24, 1975.
148 Interview with Ms. MaryLou Remley, professor of the history of athletics, Women's Athletic Department, U.W.-Madison, March 24, 1975.
149 Whyte, op. cit., p. 160.
150 Letter from Margery Latimer to Zona Gale. Undated but apparently written in 1928. All letters quoted in the sketch are on file in the Zona Gale Breese Papers in Mss. Div., WSHS.
151 Breese, Zona Gale. Obituary for Margary Latimer, The Portage Register-Democrat, August 19, 1932. All newspaper clippings on Margery Latimer were made available by the Portage Public Library.
152 "Margery Latimer," Wilson Library Bulletin, December, 1930, p. 232.
153 Ibid
154 Buss, Carl Alfred. "Margery Latimer — Wisconsin's Newest Writer," The Wisconsin Magazine, February, 1929, pp. 14-15.
155 Letter from Margery Latimer to Zona Gale, 1922. Mss. Div., WSHS.
156 Letter from Margery Latimer to Zona Gale, 1921. Mss. Div., WSHS.
157 Letter from Margery Latimer to Zona Gale, 1928. Mss. Div., WSHS.
158 Letter from Zona Gale to Margery Latimer, Spring, 1928. Mss. Div., WSHS.
159 Buss, op. cit., p. 15.
160 Breese, op. cit.
161 Buss, op. cit., p.15.
162 Griffin, Michael. "Gossips Get Thrill From Novelist's Mate," The Wisconsin State Journal, March 19, 1932. "Portage Cult Leader Sees New Race Developing," The Wisconsin News, March 18, 1932.
163 Griffin, Ibid. "Elite of Portage Shocked by Tales of Toomer Cult," The Milwaukee Sentinel, March 20, 1932. "Tongues of Portage Gossips Wag Over Toomer 'Experiment': Marriage of Writer and Poet Stirs Society Folk," The Milwaukee Sentinel, March 30, 1932. Additional information about the Portage community's reaction to Latimer's marriage was supplied by Mrs. Orilla Blackshear of Madison in an interview on November 6, 1974.
164 Letter from Margery Latimer to Zona Gale, July, 1932. Mss. Div., WSHS.

165 All information on Hildegard Chada was supplied by her daughter, Mrs. Faith Wyckoff of Salem, Oregon; and her sister, Miss Theodora Jenkel, of DePere, Wisconsin. Some of Mrs. Wyckoff's reminiscences about her mother are quoted in the sketch.

166 Anastaplo, George. "Emma Toft: Queen of the Peninsula." Talk delivered at The Clearing, Ellison Bay, Wisconsin, on August 25, 1972. pp.3-4.

167 Letter from Emma Toft, April 17, 1975. "Virgin Timber on Peninsula Not to Be Sold: Seven Heirs Stand Guard Over Striking Primeval Forest in Door County," *The Milwaukee Journal*, June 3, 1951.

168 Ibid

169 Farley, Jane Mary. "Virgin Forest Is Sanctuary to Woman Keeping Watch," *The Milwaukee Journal*, November 1, 1953.

170 Letter from Emma Toft, July 25, 1975. "Emma Toft Given Bronze Medal for Conservation," *The Door County Advocate*, September 22, 1964.

171 Farley, op. cit.

172 Ibid. Abel, Barbara. "A Legacy of Land, Preserved From 'Progress'," *Green Bay Press-Gazette*, July 10, 1966.

173 *The Door County Advocate*, op. cit. Farley, op. cit.

174 Farley, op. cit.

175 *The Door County Advocate*, op. cit. Farley, op. cit.

176 Anastalpo, op. cit., p. 4.

177 "Preserve Nature's Gifts!" *Green Bay Press-Gazette*, September 27, 1964.

178 "Emma Toft Donates Point Near Ridges to University," *The Door County Advocate*, April 23, 1968. "U.W. Given Property on Door County Shore," *Green Bay Press-Gazette*, April 19, 1968. Letter from Emma Toft, July 25, 1975. "Emma Toft Will Be Honored at UWGB," *The Door County Advocate*, May 30, 1972.

179 Butler, Genevieve. "Grass Roots." Pamphlet published in Beaver Dam, 1970.

180 Nichols, Phoebe Jewel. *Oshkosh The Brave*. Oshkosh, Wisconsin: Castle-Pierce Publishing Company; 1954. pp. 59-79.

181 Porritt, op. cit., p. 71.

182 Interview with Elizabeth Brandeis Raushenbush, Madison, May 21, 1975.

183 Bullock, Edna D. and Johnsen, Julia E., eds. *The Employment of Women*. New York: H.W. Wilson., 1920.

184 "Maud Swett to Get Award," *The Milwaukee Sentinel*, May 8, 1947.

185 Information on Maud Swett was provided by her niece, Mrs. Gladys Trayser of Madison; and by her former colleague and friend, Mrs. Elizabeth Brandeis Raushenbush of Madison.

186 Interview with E.B. Raushenbush, May 21, 1975.

187 Interview with Gladys Trayser, April 16, 1975.

188 Letter from Evelyn Doyle to Gladys Trayser, April 13, 1975.

189 The Maud Swett Papers, on file in the Mss. Div., WSHS.

190 Letter from Gladys Trayser, April 21, 1975.

191 Letter from Wagner Manufacturing Company to Maud Swett, June 20, 1956. On file in the Maud Swett Papers, Mss. Div., WSHS.

192 All information on Alma Kuhn was provided by her daughter, Mrs. Lois Hornig of Oconomowoc, Wisconsin.

193 Information on Esther Streiff Stauffacher was provided by Mrs. Frank Schiesser of New Glarus.

194 Interview with Eleanor Raasch Friedrick in Milwaukee, April 25, 1975.

195 Ibid

196 Putnam, Mabel Raef. "Do You Know About Women's Rights and the Fight for Them?" *The Wisconsin State Journal*, November, 1939.

197 Papers of the Wisconsin Society for the Equal Rights Amendment are on file in Mss. Div., WSHS.

198 Editorial, *The Capitol Times*, July 12, 1947.